The Promise

The Promise

Never have another negative thought again

Graham W Price

PEARSON

Harlow, England • London • New York • Boston • San Francisco • Toronto • Sydney
Auckland • Singapore • Hong Kong • Tokyo • Seoul • Taipei • New Delhi
Cape Town • São Paulo • Mexico City • Madrid • Amsterdam • Munich • Paris • Milan

PEARSON EDUCATION LIMITED
Edinburgh Gate
Harlow CM20 2JE
United Kingdom
Tel: +44 (0)1279 623623
Website: www.pearson.com/uk

First published 2013 (print and electronic)

Pearson Education is not responsible for the content of third-party internet sites.

ISBN: 978-0-273-78436-4 (print)
    978-0-273-78882-9 (PDF)
    978-0-273-78881-2 (ePub)

British Library Cataloguing-in-Publication Data
A catalogue record for the print edition is available from the British Library

Library of Congress Cataloging-in-Publication Data
Price, Graham W.
  The promise : never have another negative thought again / Graham Price.
    pages cm
  Includes index.
    ISBN 978-0-273-78436-4 (pbk.) -- ISBN (invalid) 978-0-273-78882-9 (PDF) -- ISBN (invalid) 978-0-273-78881-2 (ePub)
    1. Self-actualization (Psychology) 2. Positive psychology. 3. Attitude (Psychology) I. Title.
  BF637.S4P748 2013
  158--dc23
                          2012045672

10 9 8 7 6 5 4 3 2 1
17 16 15 14 13

Cover: Designed by Two Associates

Print edition typeset in 11pt Helevetica Neue LT Pro Light by 30
Print edition printed and bound in Great Britain by Henry Ling Ltd., at the Dorset Press, Dorchester, Dorset

NOTE THAT ANY PAGE CROSS REFERENCES REFER TO THE PRINT EDITION

Are you ...

- Getting all you want out of life?
- Achieving everything you want to achieve?
- Completely free of stress, regret and worry?
- Loving your work?
- Enjoying satisfying relationships?
- Waking up every morning looking forward to the day?
- Being as successful as you want to be?
- Feeling happy and confident within yourself?
- Making whatever difference in the world you'd like to make?
- Looking forward to the future?
- Able to choose the way you experience every challenging moment?

If you answered 'no' to any of these questions, this book is for you.

If you answered 'yes' to all the questions, read it anyway. It will help you encourage your friends, relations, colleagues and others to start living the exceptional life you're already enjoying.

Contents

About the author

GRAHAM W PRICE is a psychologist, therapist, stress-management consultant, relationship counsellor, personal and executive coach, personal development trainer and professional speaker. He is the developer of Acceptance-Action Therapy (AAT), Acceptance-Action Training, the techniques of Positive Acceptance and the Pacceptance Principle.

He has helped thousands to dramatically improve their lives through his unique Acceptance-Action Training and his work with individuals. His training is widely recognised as a revolutionary and highly effective approach to personal development, producing enhanced effectiveness, well-being, resilience, achievement, motivation and relationships.

Previously a general manager in one of the world's largest and most successful companies, he left the corporate world to introduce others to the ideas, tools and techniques that had substantially enhanced his own career and life.

Now a respected psychologist, coach, trainer and speaker, he has fulfilled all his goals except one … giving everyone access to these ideas. This book has been written to meet that goal.

Preface

I've written this book with one purpose in mind, to pass on to others ways of thinking and acting that have made a huge difference to my life and the lives of thousands of others I've been privileged to help and train.

My work as a therapist, coach, trainer and speaker can only reach limited numbers. It's my hope that this book will be able to influence many more lives for the better.

The pages that follow outline ways of thinking that are very different from the ways most of us have learned to think. Some of the ideas may initially seem foreign and to some even radical. It's my heartfelt hope that I've been able to convey them in a way that will dramatically improve readers' lives.

You'll need to play your part by keeping an open mind and a willingness to try new ways of thinking. Do this and these ideas, tools and techniques will open the door to an extraordinary life. That's my **promise** to you.

I'd like to thank all who've spent time reviewing the book and providing valuable input to enhance the clarity of the message it contains.

Graham W Price

BPS, BABCP, BACP, HPC, MBA, MSc

Introduction

Have you ever thought what an ideal life might look and feel like?

Would it entail being able to answer 'yes' to the questions at the beginning of this book? Perhaps for you it would need to include something more. Whatever it might involve, do you believe you can achieve such a life if you haven't already? Or do you think it's a pipe-dream, perhaps possible for others but not for you?

I truly believe it's possible for everyone. I also consider it's our right.

We've all been born into this world with the potential to live an extraordinary life. Why not realise that potential? Why settle for anything less?

Some of you may be thinking that life hasn't been all that brilliant up to now, so even if you could dramatically change it, you'd only have lived half a brilliant life. In the pages that follow you'll learn to accept the past, for the simple reason that it couldn't possibly have been different.

The future on the other hand is wide open. Wherever you are on life's journey, the future is there to be grabbed. It can be amazing. That's a **promise**.

I'll be suggesting a few exercises to illustrate some of the book's main ideas. I suggest you don't read on until you've tried each exercise. You'll only benefit from the book if you do the exercises and start to develop new thinking habits.

I'll also be using case studies, mostly from my work as a therapist, coach and stress management consultant, to demonstrate how people have put these ideas into practice. The case studies are in tinted boxes. Names and other details have been changed to protect anonymity.

At the end of each chapter you'll find a summary of suggested actions to try out the contents of that chapter, together with a summary of key actions from previous chapters.

We'll be looking at a number of ideas and it may be difficult at first to keep them all in mind at once. Each chapter will introduce at least one new idea. You may find it useful to concentrate on applying the ideas of each chapter (as well as the preceding chapters) for at least a day or two before moving on to the next. Or you may prefer to read the whole book, trying out the ideas as you go, then revisit the chapter summaries, focusing on each summary for a few days before moving onto the next.

Look out for opportunities to put the ideas into practice in your daily life. Observe the way others think and behave either directly or through television or any other medium and imagine how you might have thought or acted in the same situation with the ideas discussed in this book.

Spend a few minutes at the end of each day reviewing the day in the light of the latest action summary, including actions from prior chapters, and consider whether you've used, or could have used, all the relevant tools and techniques.

CHAPTER 1

Positive acceptance

"The greatest discovery of our generation is that a person can change his life by altering his attitude of mind."
WILLIAM JAMES

I probably shouldn't start by offending all my readers, but I have to tell you the truth. You're crazy. Actually, completely bonkers. The fact is we're all crazy. There may be some exceptions, but truly I doubt if you're one of them.

Let me explain.

Think of a time when you've been unhappy, dissatisfied, disappointed, stressed or irritated about something. Maybe you were chastising yourself when you left the house and shut the door with the keys still inside. Perhaps you were annoyed with your local council when they got you to separate all your recyclables, then tipped everything in the same truck.

Well, here's an extraordinary fact about us humans. Whenever we're dissatisfied about anything, we're nearly always wanting the past or present moment to be different, which is wishing for the impossible.

We all know the past can never be changed, though you may at times still wish it were different. Perhaps you haven't thought so much about the fact that the present moment can never be changed either. We may be able to change the next moment or any future moment, but we can never undo what already is.

And yet that's what we're nearly always wanting, whenever we're dissatisfied about anything. We're either wanting something that's happened not to have happened, or we're wanting a situation that exists right now not to exist right now. Both are wishing for the impossible.

Now, that's what I call crazy.

I say 'nearly always', because there's an exception – worrying about the future. We'll look at worry later and I'll try to persuade you this is just as crazy.

For the moment let's stick with the main evidence for my claim. We humans spend a great deal of time and energy wishing things were already different, in other words wanting the past or present moment to be different, such as:

- Regretting something we've done or haven't done
- Being unhappy, dissatisfied or stressed about something that's happened or a situation that exists right now
- Wishing we already have more abilities, more confidence, better health, more wealth, than we currently have
- Being unhappy about, or complaining (unproductively) about, other people's actions

In all these cases, we're effectively wanting something to be already different, which is crazy because nothing can ever be already different.

What if we could accept the past and present moment all the time, and at the same time develop our abilities to change whatever we want to change and achieve whatever we want to achieve in the next moment or the future?

What if, having left the house, closed the door and realised the keys are still inside, we could immediately accept the situation (not wish it were already different) and think only about how to rectify it and prevent it happening again?

What if having watched the refuse collector tip our separated rubbish in the same truck, we could immediately accept the situation (not wish it were already different) and think only about whether there's something we can reasonably do towards preventing it happening again?

What if we could do this with every challenging situation we ever face?

Some of you may think you already do this, in which case I wholeheartedly apologise for suggesting you're crazy. But let me ask you. Be honest. Are you ever unhappy, dissatisfied, disappointed, stressed or irritated about anything? If you are then you're at least occasionally wanting something to be already different. So maybe you're just a bit crazy.

ACCEPTING WHAT IS

The word 'acceptance' is most commonly used to imply consenting to something, resigning ourselves to a situation, or not trying to change things.

This type of acceptance means not wanting something to be different in the future. This makes sense when we're accepting things we cannot possibly change. But this isn't the type of acceptance I'm talking about here.

I'm talking about not wanting something to be **already** different. This can be applied to every challenging situation, whether or not we can change it. The term we use for this is 'accepting what is'.

Accepting what is, means accepting the past or present moment. It means recognising we cannot undo what already is. So there's no point wishing that something that's happened, or a situation that exists right now, were already different.

The opposite of 'accepting what is', is 'resisting what is', which is another term for wanting something to be already different. Resisting what is, is the source of practically all unhappiness and dissatisfaction.

Accepting what is, enables us to focus on what we need to do to change the situation for the better or otherwise improve the future.

If I've failed an exam, there's no point dwelling on how much better it would be if I'd passed, wishing I'd worked harder, had more ability or been luckier with the questions. I'll be happier if I can accept what's happened, for the simple reason that it's happened and cannot be 'unhappened', and concentrate on whatever needs to be done to improve the future: work harder, change direction or whatever.

What if we could learn to accept what is all the time? Maybe life would be different. For now, if you haven't already adopted this way of thinking, you'll have to take my word for it – it's very different.

CASE STUDY

Many years ago, when I knew nothing about 'accepting what is' (in fact I knew very little about anything really worth knowing), I witnessed a middle-ranking executive face a career-threatening challenge.

On the spur of the moment, he produced a response that impressed everyone who witnessed it.

When I later congratulated him for what he'd done, he took the time to give me some advice. He said he believed it was the best advice he could give anyone. He said, 'When you're facing a challenging situation, don't waste a moment wishing it were different. Just focus on how you can make it different.'

At first I thought, surely we have to want something to be different to be motivated to change it. Then I realised we only have to want something to be different in the next moment or the future to be motivated to change it. What he meant was 'don't waste a moment wishing it were already different'.

He wasn't 'accepting' the situation, since he clearly intended to change it. But he was 'accepting what is'.

At the time I still initially thought that, while sensible, this seemed a rather obvious piece of wisdom. But I quickly realised that, however sensible and obvious it might seem, it wasn't a piece of wisdom I was following in my life. When I stopped to think about it, I noticed I was wanting situations to be already different many times every day.

I soon realised that practically everyone else seemed to be doing the same.

The executive who gave me this advice was one of the most effective, focused and unflappable individuals I've ever met. He went on to become the chief executive of one of the world's largest and most successful companies.

So how could we drop our habit of resisting what is or wanting things to be already different, replacing it with accepting what is, then focusing on action to change it if that's what we want to do?

What if whenever we're dissatisfied about anything, we could make ourselves aware that what we're doing is wanting something to be already different? In other words we're wishing the past or present moment were different.

What if we could acknowledge that this is irrational (actually crazy!) because nothing can be already different, so we're wishing for the impossible?

Maybe we could then drop the thought and refocus on what we can do, if anything, to make it different in the next moment or the future.

You may question whether you can drop such thoughts. The truth is that when we realise a thought is irrational and of no benefit, we can drop it, except when we're experiencing strong emotions. If you doubt you can do this, I suggest you give it a try.

Don't start with your big issue if you have one. Start small and build up:

■ The train has just left and you're still on the platform

■ You want to make a mobile call and the battery's flat

■ You've planned something outdoors and it's raining

If we're dissatisfied with any of these situations or any other situation, we're 'resisting what is'. The situation is what it is. It cannot be already different so we may as well drop any thought that involves wishing it were and refocus on what we can do, if anything, to make it different or improve the future.

As you're looking at the rain with irritation or disappointment at having to change your outdoor plans, recognise you're wanting something to be already different, acknowledge you're wishing for the impossible, choose to drop the thought and refocus on what you can do to improve the situation. Move your plans indoors, order a marquee, go scuba diving.

We're not just trying to turn off negative thoughts: On its own that would be pretty challenging. The key is to recognise we're wishing something were already different and that this is irrational. With that realisation, we can usually drop the thought once any emotional reaction has subsided and refocus on what we need to do, if anything, to improve the future.

And we're not talking about trying to force negative thoughts out of our mind. This is virtually impossible.

Exercise

Imagine a pink elephant. See the image clearly in your mind. Now stop reading and think for the next 10 seconds about anything except a pink elephant. Don't on any account think of a pink elephant.

I expect you found this pretty challenging. By contrast, letting go of a thought is something we can do when we realise it's irrational and of no benefit. We can then replace it with thoughts of how we can improve the future. My guess is you've now stopped thinking about the pink elephant.

POSITIVE ACCEPTANCE

Our suggested technique for developing a habit of accepting what is, and then refocusing on action to change the future, needs a name.

We initially called it 'positive acceptance'. As this proved a bit of a mouthful, especially when used as a verb, popular usage led to its abbreviation, taking the 'p' out of 'positive' and creating the word 'pacceptance'.

For the moment, the technique we're proposing for paccepting something is:

- Notice that we're wishing something were already different (practically always the case whenever we're dissatisfied about anything)
- Recognise that this is an irrational thought (nothing can be already different, so we're wishing for the impossible)
- Drop the thought
- Refocus on what we can do, if anything, to improve the future

The first three steps are about 'accepting what is'. The fourth is about refocusing on action.

What if we could develop a habit of paccepting whenever we're unhappy or dissatisfied about anything? Thousands of people have found it to be life changing, so it might be worth a try.

CASE STUDY

Sophie was enjoying life when she came to one of my seminars. She had no particular issues but had heard about Positive Acceptance and was curious to know what it was. She found the idea appealing and started using it.

Like a great many others before and since, she sent me a message saying she'd immediately found herself using pacceptance a dozen times a day. She said the impact on her life was dramatic.

When I met her again some time later, she reported, as have most others, that her use of pacceptance had become more automatic. Still later she noticed that thoughts involving 'wishing things were already different' were arising less often.

So far we've only been talking about paccepting our circumstances. In the third chapter we'll be applying it to our feelings.

There really aren't too many things in life that we need to accept in the sense of acknowledging there's nothing we can do to change them in the future. But if we want to rid our lives of dissatisfaction, we could develop a habit of paccepting everything whenever we find ourselves with a thought that involves wishing something were already different.

THE PACCEPTANCE PRINCIPLE

And if we want to change something in the future we won't achieve it by wishing. We won't improve our lot in life by wishing we were better off. We won't improve the world we live in by wishing people behaved differently. We won't develop our abilities by wishing we had more abilities. If we want to change something in the future we need to do something to make it happen.

The pacceptance principle ... is simply this:

> *What is, is*
> *And there's no point wishing*
> *That what is, isn't*
> *But if there's something we want to*
> *change or achieve*
> *And it's within our power to change or*
> *achieve it*
> *We won't do it by wishing; we need*
> *to act*

So when we paccept something, we can refocus on how we can make it different in the future, if that's what we want and are able to do.

You may have misjudged something that's resulted in a costly mistake. Paccepting what's happened doesn't mean ignoring your responsibility, the need to make amends or the importance of preventing a recurrence. It just means choosing not to spend time and energy wishing it hadn't happened and refocusing your thoughts on improving the future rather than regretting the past.

CASE STUDY

When I met Jim, his building business was failing; he had some big debts; his wife was threatening to leave him and one of his teenage children was mixing with a group that was having a negative influence on her life. Jim felt powerless to intervene.

When Jim learned about pacceptance, he initially tried to apply it to all his issues at once. I encouraged him to practise on smaller things first, such as day-to-day issues as they arose.

After a while, he was able to start applying it to the bigger issues in his life. Whenever he found himself wishing his situation was already different, he'd use the pacceptance technique.

He quickly became less dissatisfied and more oriented towards action. After a while his dissatisfaction disappeared and he was taking stronger action to address each of his issues.

Jim's view of his situation became very different, and as he applied the other techniques outlined in this book, his life started to change dramatically.

Here's a summary of the definitions we've used so far:

- **Acceptance** means not wanting something to be different in the future. Hence traditional wisdom encourages us to accept the things we cannot change. Acceptance is not a particularly useful concept in most situations.

- **Accepting what is** means not wanting something to be already different. We can apply this to any situation, whether or not we can change it, because whenever we're dissatisfied about anything we're nearly always wanting something to be already different.

- **Pacceptance** is a four-step process that helps us develop a habit of accepting what is combined with refocusing on action to improve the future. We'll benefit enormously if we develop a habit of paccepting whenever we're dissatisfied about anything. If there's no action we can or want to take, we can just apply the first three steps of the process.

OUR REACTIONS

Does this mean we shouldn't react to unwelcome situations with disappointment, annoyance or frustration? Not at all. These reactions are perfectly normal.

What we do when we react may not be so desirable or unavoidable. But for the moment, I'm just talking about the thinking and feeling part of our reactions.

There's nothing wrong with the thoughts and feelings that make up our reactions. Even though some reactions such as fear and frustration may be uncomfortable, there usually isn't much we can immediately do to avoid them. (We can remove them from our lives eventually if we want to, and we'll see how later.)

To understand why we can't immediately change our reactions, we need to spend a moment looking at where they come from.

We've each learned or developed all sorts of expectations or preferences as to how the world should be, what we should be experiencing, and how we or others should behave.

We naturally tend to compare these expectations, often unconsciously, with what's happening. When the comparisons are unfavourable, we may feel disappointed, annoyed, frustrated or upset. Our feelings and the automatic thoughts that trigger them are controlled by our unconscious programming, which is the way our unconscious mind thinks or reacts. Some of this programming is handed down genetically, such as fear reactions when faced with danger, while some is learned, mainly during childhood.

As we don't have immediate control over our unconscious mind, we generally don't have direct control over our feelings or the automatic thoughts that trigger them. Usually we can't immediately change the thoughts and feelings that make up our reactions. Over time we can and we'll see how later.

Far from trying to immediately change our feelings, we'll be talking in the third chapter about the huge value of accepting them.

Our initial reactions usually subside fairly quickly. If we then keep thinking about the situation in a negative way, we'll simply remain dissatisfied and perpetuate or keep repeating our reaction. It may even take on a more extended form such as anger turning into resentment.

But if, when any initial reaction has subsided, we can choose to paccept what is, we'll avoid perpetuating the thoughts that generated our reaction in the first place. After all, it isn't our reactions that cause most dissatisfaction in life. Our reactions tend to be short-lived and account for only a small fraction of all our thoughts and feelings.

> *Most dissatisfaction arises when we perpetuate thoughts that entail wishing something were already different.*

FOR INSTANCE

I'm travelling by train to an important meeting. The train breaks down and I realise I'm going to be late. My expectations or preferences as to how the world should be right now include trains not breaking down, at least when I'm on them, and me not being late for important meetings.

I'll probably automatically compare my situation with these expectations and react with frustration, annoyance, disappointment or worry. I might even start thinking about all the possible consequences of my lateness and so add to my unhappiness.

But if I can make myself aware that what I'm doing is wishing something were already different then, once any initial reaction has subsided, I can choose to change my thinking.

The train has broken down. I am going to be late.

> *What is, is, and there's no point wishing that what is, isn't.*

I can choose to paccept the situation.

CASE STUDY

Michael had been diagnosed with cancer some months before I met him. He'd been devastated by the news. When we met he was both determined and hopeful that he could beat it, yet at the same time he was very troubled.

When I mentioned 'acceptance', he responded 'acceptance is fine for the things you can't change, but I'm going to beat this, so it's not for me'.

When I explained the difference between acceptance and 'accepting what is' he saw the value of 'accepting what is' and realised it didn't conflict with his desire and determination to beat his cancer.

He started using pacceptance and found that it settled his troubled state and enabled him to focus more on what he needed to do to win his battle.

He did win and later said he believed his use of pacceptance had been a major factor.

DEVELOPING THE HABIT

What we're talking about is a radically different way of thinking about countless minor situations we encounter daily and major situations we may confront periodically in our lives. Adopting this way of thinking has a hugely beneficial impact.

Many people are generally aware of the wisdom of accepting the things we cannot change, but may not always use it. You're no doubt aware that the past cannot be changed and that it makes sense to accept what's already happened, but you may not have developed a habit of always thinking this way.

Most people aren't aware of the concept of accepting the present moment, and hence the idea of pacceptance, and so are unlikely to have ever tried it.

I do sometimes meet people who are familiar with the wisdom of 'accepting what is' but don't have a tool for routinely achieving this and so haven't developed it as a habit in their lives.

> *Our failure to accept what is, while refocusing on action to improve the future, is responsible for almost all the unhappiness or dissatisfaction we may experience.*

If you doubt you can choose your thoughts in this way, I urge you to give it a try. Start with small events and build up once you've mastered the process.

Next time the traffic lights are red when you're running late, you've just burned the toast, the kids have put mud on the carpet or anything else has happened that's disappointed, annoyed, frustrated or upset you, try choosing to paccept the situation once any initial reaction has subsided.

The extent to which we're willing to incorporate this simple practice into our lives can be a major determinant of the satisfaction or dissatisfaction we'll experience during our lifetime.

PACCEPTANCE IS EMPOWERING

Because pacceptance changes our focus from what's wrong to what we can do about it, it changes us from feeling powerless to feeling empowered.

CASE STUDY

Soon after I first started using pacceptance I found myself, as in the above example, running late for an important meeting. I was feeling frustrated by every hold-up and was chastising myself for not leaving earlier.

I realised that every thought that was running through my mind entailed wishing my situation were already different. I applied pacceptance and eliminated those unhelpful thoughts.

When I came to thinking about action to improve the future, I realised 'running late for meetings' had become a pattern in my life. I made a commitment to always leave 20 minutes earlier, or more if appropriate, for every important meeting from then on.

Not only did I stop running late for meetings, but making this commitment gave me an immediate sense of being in control of my life at that moment instead of feeling powerless.

Pacceptance can be applied to the present or the past and a similar process can be applied to the future to eliminate worry.

THE PRESENT

Our attitude towards inconvenience, discomfort, disappointment or any other source of dissatisfaction can be radically changed through practising pacceptance.

If you're stuck in a lift, are suffering from an illness or have just broken your favourite possession, you can paccept the situation once any initial reaction has subsided, even though you might prefer it were different. Then you can get on with doing whatever you need to do and are able to do, if anything, to improve the future.

CASE STUDY

Paul is a self-employed consultant. He came to see me because he was constantly stressed by his work.

Sometimes he had too much work and was stressed by the thought that he wouldn't be able to satisfy all his customers. Sometimes he had too little work and was stressed by the thought that he wouldn't be able to sustain his income.

And he found himself upset by day-to-day occurrences, such as being let down by a supplier who'd promised a piece of work and hadn't delivered on time or on quality.

He knew about the wisdom of 'accepting the things you cannot change' but, like so many others I've helped, he felt he should be able to control the things he was stressed about and so didn't see any value in accepting them.

He'd never heard about 'accepting what is'. He took to it straight away and started using pacceptance in his work and in other aspects of his life.

His stress level immediately diminished, and when he learned about other techniques discussed in this book it disappeared completely.

Exercise

Spend a few moments thinking about something you're not entirely satisfied with, or that you wish were different. Preferably choose something relatively minor for now, rather than the big issue in your life (if you have one).

Try to choose something you don't blame yourself or anyone else for, as we'll be looking at blame in a later chapter.

Whatever it is, consider the difference between wishing it were already different and wanting it to be different in the future.

Acknowledge that if you're dissatisfied about it, you're almost certainly wishing it were **already** different, which is wishing for the impossible.

Choose to 'accept what is', i.e. drop any thought that involves wanting it to be already different, and re-focus on what can be done, if anything, to improve the future.

THE PAST

You can remove regret from your life through pacceptance, whether it's regret about something that's happened, or something you've done or haven't done.

Maybe it would have been better not to have said whatever we said. There may well have been opportunities in our lives we didn't take. These are worth thinking about if this can help us or others to avoid repeating them. But regret adds nothing of value and is usually just debilitating and self-limiting.

Whenever we have a thought that includes the words 'if only', we can choose to replace it with pacceptance. 'If only I'd studied more when I was younger.' 'If only I'd started my journey earlier.' 'If only I'd done what was needed to be richer, healthier, thinner or more confident.'

These thoughts have no value, except to the extent that they encourage us to do something different in the future. We can choose to replace them with pacceptance.

Exercise

Think about something you regret, perhaps something you did that you wish you hadn't done, perhaps a missed opportunity.

Recognise that if you're regretting it, you're effectively wishing something were **already** different, which is wishing for the impossible.

Choose to paccept it, i.e. drop the thought that involves wishing it were already different, and refocus on what can be done, if anything, to improve the future.

There are some situations where it may **not** be helpful to try to change our non-paccepting thoughts. If we're grieving over the loss of a loved one or any other significant loss, we need time to work through these thoughts and feelings.

Trying to change our thoughts in this instance may not be helpful unless we've been grieving an abnormally long time. But accepting the feelings involved in grief can be enormously helpful (as we'll see in Chapter 3).

There are also some situations involving our own or other people's behaviour that can be difficult to paccept if at the same time we're blaming ourselves or others for something we or they have done. We'll introduce a more powerful approach for dealing with regret and blame in Chapter 5, 'An extraordinary truth'.

THE FUTURE

Following the pacceptance principle generally means accepting the past and present moment and taking action to influence the future. But we can apply a related form of acceptance to the future and so remove worry from our lives. We'll cover this in the next chapter.

WHAT IF THE NEGATIVE THOUGHT RETURNS?

Then just apply pacceptance again. It's an opportunity to practise the technique. This may well happen initially, but in time and with practice it will diminish and finally disappear.

In fact when you've practised pacceptance for a while, you'll find not only do the negative thoughts stop returning, they arise less in the first place. When we retrain our conscious ways of thinking, this soon starts to impact our automatic or unconscious ways of thinking.

ISN'T DISSATISFACTION A MOTIVATOR?

Some might ask whether we aren't more motivated to act when we're dissatisfied. I used to think so. But I, and the many others I know who regularly practise pacceptance, haven't found it to be so.

Most unhappiness and dissatisfaction are debilitating rather than motivating. We're much better served by motivations based on purpose, commitment, preference, contribution and awareness of the benefits of change. In the long run, these are a lot more productive than motivations based on resentment, regret, worry and discontent.

When you remove regret, dissatisfaction and worry from your life you can make the most of the here and now and contribute more to the future, instead of being unhappy about the past or present or worried about the future.

WOULDN'T LIFE BE RATHER DULL IF WE'RE NEVER DISSATISFIED?

It turns out the opposite is true. When we adopt pacceptance as a way of thinking, life becomes far more enjoyable and satisfying. The gap that's left by removing dissatisfaction is filled by fun, contribution and a desire to explore possibilities and make the most of life.

And when we apply it to our uncomfortable feelings, the emotional aspects of life become fuller and more satisfying as well (as we'll discuss in Chapter 3).

Action summary

- Whenever you find yourself dissatisfied with anything, once any emotional reaction has subsided, **paccept** it:

  - **Recognise** you're wishing something were already different

  - **Acknowledge** this is an irrational thought; nothing can be already different, so you're wishing for the impossible

  - **Drop** the thought

  - **Refocus** on what you can do, if anything, to improve the future, such as changing the situation or preventing it happening again.

- **Start small** and build up to bigger things

- Think about any **regrets** and apply pacceptance to them

- **Observe** non-pacceptance in others (TV, etc.) and consider how you'd now think and act in their circumstances

CHAPTER 2

Banning worry

"Worry is a word I don't allow myself to use." DWIGHT EISENHOWER

Now that we've dealt with 'resisting what is', including 'resisting what was', we need to turn our attention to 'resisting what will be'.

We've said that practically all dissatisfaction entails wanting something to be **already** different. The only exception is worrying about the future. Worry is about 'resisting the future', otherwise called 'resisting what will be' or more accurately, in most cases, 'resisting what may be'.

There's nothing wrong with wanting the future to be different. In fact the final step of the pacceptance process involves precisely that ... thinking about how we want the future to be and doing whatever we can to achieve it. But worrying about the future achieves nothing.

We define worry as 'ruminating about a negative outcome'. So when we're worrying we have an image of something bad happening in the future ... **and** we believe we cannot control it. If we believed we could control it, we wouldn't be worrying.

Wanting something to be different in the future, from the way we think it may be, when we believe we have no control over the outcome is about as futile as wishing something were **already** different.

The only thing that does make sense is to think about how we can better determine the future and gain more control over whatever it is we're worrying about. And, to the extent we're not able to do this, we need to accept whatever the future might be.

Accept what we cannot control and focus on improving what we can control. This is what we need to do if we want to rid our lives of worry.

We can practise this in the same way that we practiced 'accepting what is', using a four-step process similar to pacceptance:

1 Create a habit of noticing whenever you're worrying
2 Recognise this is an irrational thought. You're want-ing something to be a certain way in the future **and** you believe you have no control over it
3 Drop the worrying thought
4 Refocus on how you can gain more control over whatever you were worrying about or otherwise improve the future

If there's genuinely nothing you can think of doing to gain more control, then stop after step 3.

You may find the worrying thought returns. Fine. Just see that as an opportunity to practise the process again.

It helps to practise pacceptance (of the past and present), as outlined in the first chapter, for a while, before trying to apply the equivalent process to worry.

CASE STUDY

Ingrid was in her mid-50s and by most people's standards her life was in pretty good shape. She had a good job, a loving husband and her grown-up children were making their way in the world.

But Ingrid had a problem. She wasn't coping well with getting older. She'd lost some of her youthful looks, was feeling less healthy, had put on weight and was becoming more agitated by her advancing age and the prospect of one day growing 'old'.

She'd tried to focus on the positive aspects of her life, but couldn't keep her mind from returning to what she saw as her 'big issue'. When I introduced her to pacceptance, she at first found it difficult to apply to her problem.

But she started applying it to other areas of her life, initially relatively minor day-to-day events, then some bigger issues such as regrets involving missed opportunities.

Within a short time, as she became more paccepting, she was able to fully paccept herself, her age, her changing appearance and the process of growing older.

She started taking action in the areas she could control. She joined a health club, lost weight and began to feel a lot healthier and more vibrant.

PACCEPTING OUTCOMES

In the last chapter we introduced pacceptance as a vehicle to train ourselves to 'accept what is' all the time. Once we've developed the ability to paccept everything then we can be confident that whatever happens in the future, we'll be able to paccept it.

Before I achieved this, I used to believe that one thing I'd find hard to cope with would be a disability. While I wouldn't ever wish it on myself or anyone else, I no longer believe I'd find it so hard to cope, were it ever to happen. I've become so used to paccepting everything that I now believe I'd be able to paccept disability, along with everything else that I routinely paccept. Since I cannot think of anything else much worse that could happen, I now feel comfortable about my ability to paccept anything that may happen.

Once you know you can paccept anything, what is there left to worry about?

EXAGGERATION

The tools above are used in Acceptance-Action Training or Acceptance-Action Therapy (AAT) for dealing with worry. The following is a Cognitive-Behavioural Therapy (CBT) approach.

Whenever we're worrying, we're nearly always exaggerating one or both of two things:

1 The probability of something bad happening

2 The consequences, even if that 'something' were to happen

Identifying those exaggerations will enable us to view whatever we're worrying about from a more realistic perspective.

CASE STUDY

Back in the days when I used to get anxious about speaking to groups, I worried whenever I had a speaking engagement approaching. I was no doubt worried some disaster might occur.

I was certainly exaggerating the probability of such a disaster. After all I'd survived several times already, so the chances were pretty reasonable I'd get through it again without any disaster occurring.

I was also exaggerating the consequences even if the feared 'disaster' were to occur. If I'd stumbled as a result of losing my way or becoming overly anxious, would that have been the end of the world as I imagined it would?

Quite probably the audience would have been empathic as most of them were, or had been, anxious about speaking to groups. Quite probably they'd have forgotten about it pretty quickly and life would have gone on as before.

Realising this, together with the pacceptance-based approaches already described, eliminated my worry about speaking to groups. However, I still felt anxious on the day, and we'll see how this was resolved in the next two chapters.

CHOOSE WHAT WORKS

Some find the pacceptance-based approaches to be effective. Others have found identifying exaggerations to be effective. I suggest you try both and use the one that works best for you.

'WHAT IF' QUESTIONS

A great deal of worrying involves asking the question 'what if …?' 'What if I don't succeed in this challenge?' 'What if we run out of money?' When we find ourselves asking 'what if' questions in a worrying way, we can replace them with 'then what' thinking. 'If this was to happen, then we'd …'

For example, 'If I don't succeed in this challenge, then by using the tools in this book I'll probably succeed next time.'

WORRY IS FUTILE

It helps to recognise that worry is futile and has no value. Some believe worry can be helpful as it focuses our mind on the problem. Thinking about a problem so we can come up with a solution is fine. But we don't call that worry. We're defining worry as 'ruminating about a negative outcome'. Thinking about a solution is valuable. Ruminating about a possible negative outcome isn't.

Awareness of how we want the future to be and making plans are sufficient without needing to worry.

> *Worry focuses on the problem.*
> *Pacceptance focuses on the solution.*

PUTTING IT IN PERSPECTIVE

Most of the things we worry about never happen. And even if they don't immediately turn out the way we'd prefer, they generally work out all right in the end.

What's more, most of the things we worry about aren't so serious that we couldn't adapt even if the worst were to happen. We've survived this far after all.

If you do find yourself worrying it may help to ask:

- What's the worst that could happen?
- If that was to happen, then what would happen?
- Then what would happen? (repeat a few times)
- Even if all this were to happen would I or anyone else I'm worrying about still be alive?
- Would we ever be able to smile or laugh again?

You may not get through all the questions before you begin to see the problem in its true perspective and realise there aren't too many things really worth worrying about.

It's also worth remembering that worry is just a thought; it isn't reality.

> *Pacceptance focuses on reality by encouraging us to accept what is, or accept what will be to the extent we cannot control it.*

A popular form of worry is worrying about the possible consequences of something we've already done, a sort of worry–regret cocktail:

- 'Am I going to get there on time or should I have left earlier?'
- 'Will the job I've taken work out all right or should I have taken the other one?'

Whatever we've done is done. Whatever has happened has happened. Whatever the outcome may be, with practice we'll be able to paccept it. So we may as well stop worrying. It's simply a matter of choosing to do just that.

Exercise

Spend a few moments reflecting on some of the things you've worried about in the past and see whether your fears were realised.

On the rare occasion they were, ask yourself whether it really turned out so badly after all.

If you repeatedly use the tools outlined in this chapter and summarised below, you can eliminate worry from your life. That's a **promise**.

You may need to be tough on yourself and refuse to maintain a worrying thought by using these tools.

Action summary

If you find yourself **worrying**, try the following and find which approaches work best for you:

■ Apply the **pacceptance** technique to the future (create a habit of noticing when you're worrying; recognise worry is irrational as there's no point wishing something were different if you believe you can't control it; drop any worrying thoughts; and refocus on what you can do, if anything, to improve the future)

- Realise that with practice **you'll always be able to paccept** whatever happens
- Recognise you're almost certainly **exaggerating**:
  - The probability of something happening, and/or
  - The consequences even if it does happen
- Replace **'what-ifs'** with 'then-whats'
- Understand worry serves **no useful purpose** that isn't already served by thinking about, being concerned about, or planning for, the future
- **Focus on the solution**, not the problem
- Recognise worry is **just a thought**, not reality

Prior chapters:

- **Paccept** what is (our circumstances) at every opportunity
- **Observe** non-pacceptance in others (TV, etc.) and consider how you'd now think and act in their circumstances

CHAPTER 3

Those trying feelings

"The best way out is through." ROBERT FROST

In the first two chapters our aim was to change the way we think about uncomfortable circumstances. In this chapter, we'll be looking to change the way we think about uncomfortable feelings.

Sometime fairly early in life, most of us developed the notion that it somehow isn't OK to experience uncomfortable feelings.

If we're feeling sad, depressed, lonely, hurt, anxious, rejected, fearful or embarrassed and we're wishing we weren't feeling that way or thinking we 'shouldn't' be feeling that way (which is how most of us have learned to think), we're unwittingly involved in a highly unproductive way of thinking.

This perfectly normal but hugely unhelpful way of thinking arises partly from our quite natural desire to avoid anything painful or uncomfortable. But there's more to it than that. There are plenty of other uncomfortable experiences that don't give us the same sense of unease. Why are we so uncomfortable about uncomfortable feelings?

Perhaps we view them as a sign of weakness or think others might see them that way.

Maybe it's a result of others trying to make us feel better when we were upset as a child. Our parents or others may have made suggestions such as 'don't cry'. By trying to make us feel better when we weren't feeling good, they may have unwittingly given us an impression that it's not OK to feel whatever we're feeling.

Another possibility is that the behaviour that sometimes results from a child's feelings, such as anger or jealousy, may reasonably be viewed by adults as undesirable or unacceptable. But the adult's communication usually fails to distinguish between the behaviour, which may need to be restrained, and the underlying feelings, which never need be restrained. So the child develops the notion that the feelings themselves are undesirable or unacceptable and unconsciously carries this into adulthood.

It's worth mentioning that one of the most valuable things any parent can do for their children is to validate their feelings; to make it clear that it's OK to feel whatever they're feeling. If you didn't do this as a parent, don't worry. How could you have known if no one told you? Your parents probably didn't know either. In Chapter 5 you'll be able to let go of any concerns about what you did or didn't do, within reason, as a parent.

Whatever the explanation of our aversion to uncomfortable feelings, the notion that such feelings aren't always OK is a particularly unhelpful one.

> *Our feelings are always OK, for now.*

Since we don't have direct control over our unconscious mind, there's no point wishing we weren't feeling whatever we're feeling. On the contrary, we'll benefit hugely if we can learn to accept our uncomfortable feelings as long as they're there.

NOT HARMFUL

It's worth knowing that feelings are always harmless, however uncomfortable they may seem at the time. Nobody has ever been harmed by a feeling.

We may be harmed by what we do as a result of a feeling. People who are depressed or angry may harm themselves or others. But the feeling itself is harmless.

We may be harmed by the source of a feeling, but the feeling itself is a harmless messaging system. Cold can harm us. But feeling cold is just a message to the brain to let us know there's a problem. The feeling itself is harmless.

ACCEPTING 'FOR NOW'

Our aim is still to diminish uncomfortable feelings as soon as we can. So when I talk about accepting them, I don't mean it's OK to still be experiencing them five minutes, five hours or five days from now. I'm just talking about accepting them for now, as long as we're experiencing them.

> *It's OK for now to feel annoyed,*
> *nervous, depressed, lonely, anxious*
> *or whatever else we're feeling.*
> *What is, is and there's no point wishing*
> *that what is, isn't.*

For most, this is no small change in the way we think. It's a dramatic change with correspondingly huge benefits.

CASE STUDY

Kiera's life was dominated by feelings. She'd been in a car accident several months before I met her. She was in constant pain and wasn't sleeping well and so was perpetually tired.

She'd become anxious following the accident and was experiencing regular panic attacks. Her moods seemed uncontrollable, sometimes becoming irritated with her family for no apparent reason, often spontaneously bursting into tears.

Finally the strain of dealing with all her discomfort and the practical difficulties of life following the accident had led to her becoming depressed.

In therapy we were able to resolve all her feelings using the approaches outlined in this book, except the pain, which she learned to manage until medical and physical interventions could resolve that too.

But we were only able to successfully address her feelings once she'd learned to accept them.

Acceptance of her pain allowed her to sleep better. Acceptance of her anxiety, depression, irritation and tearfulness diminished her anguish about each of those feelings and, as we shall see, allowed her to take the actions necessary to resolve them.

LESS UNHAPPY ABOUT OUR FEELINGS

The first and most obvious benefit of accepting uncomfortable feelings is that, while it may not be pleasant to experience them, the effect on our happiness is immediately diminished if we can accept them as long as we have them.

If we're feeling low and we can accept that it's OK to feel that way for now, we'll be less unhappy than if we were wishing we weren't feeling low.

If there's something we can do to diminish the feeling, so much the better. In fact if the feeling persists we need to do something. But until we can take action to resolve the feeling, or if it's just a short-term feeling anyway, we can accept that there's nothing wrong with feeling this way for now, even if we may 'prefer' that we didn't.

And, as we shall see, for many uncomfortable feelings acceptance is often the most effective way of diminishing or resolving them.

ACCEPT OR PACCEPT?

I tend to talk about accepting rather than paccepting feelings since we cannot immediately change them and it makes sense to accept the things we cannot change. We could equally use the term 'paccept' since the key is to stop wishing we weren't feeling whatever we're feeling right now.

OBSERVING OUR FEELINGS

Being human inevitably involves experiencing a whole range of feelings so when we experience uncomfortable feelings we can accept them as simply part of being human.

> *When we start accepting our uncomfortable feelings life becomes a great deal easier.*

Accepting them allows us to view them more objectively.

Instead of our thoughts being automatically embroiled in whatever we're feeling, we can just observe the feeling. We can be aware of it without becoming wrapped up in it. If we think of our feelings as waves on an ocean, we can ride up and down on the waves and notice they're there without becoming engulfed by them.

To make an analogy, if I have a sore finger and I identify myself totally with my finger and the pain, then it's 'I' that's in pain and 'I' that's suffering. But if I can look on my 'self' as being primarily my thoughts or the part of me that's doing the observing and thinking, then I can see my 'self' separately from my sore finger.

This way I'll still feel the pain but I can view it in a more detached way. I can view it more objectively and at the deeper level that I identify as my 'self' my mental anguish or suffering is diminished. This is a key approach in helping people to manage chronic pain.

In the same way we can look on uncomfortable feelings more objectively and so diminish our suffering. Instead of seeing myself as being depressed, I can see myself as feeling depressed with my 'self' observing and accepting the feeling.

FULLY EXPERIENCING THE FEELING

There are two steps involved in accepting uncomfortable feelings. The first is to focus on and fully experience the feeling. To many this may sound strange if we've spent much of our lives trying to avoid experiencing uncomfortable feelings. Focusing on a feeling and fully experiencing it stops us trying to avoid it.

The second step is to ask ourselves: 'What's so bad about this feeling? Is it so bad that I can't accept it for now?' Then accept it, saying to ourselves: 'It's OK to have this feeling for now.'

Try this exercise:

Exercise

Next time you're in the shower turn down the hot water just enough so you start to feel uncomfortable. Examine the feeling you're experiencing.

Recognise that it's just cool(ish) water hitting your skin and giving you an uncomfortable sensation. Focus on the feeling and fully experience it.

Ask yourself whether it's doing you any harm. It isn't. No one has ever been harmed by a feeling.

Ask yourself whether you can bear the feeling. Providing you haven't made the water unbearably cold, tell yourself that you can bear it. In fact the only feeling I would say is truly unbearable is extreme pain.

Finally ask yourself: 'If this feeling isn't harming me, and I can bear it, what exactly is the problem with having the feeling right now other than the fact that it's uncomfortable?' Say to yourself. 'I can accept this feeling for now even though I might prefer that it doesn't stay around for too long.'

If you're reading this on a cold winter's day you can do the exercise right now by walking outside under-dressed.

If you can accept an externally generated feeling such as cold, then in the same way you can accept internally generated feelings such as anxiety, sadness or feeling low. Just ask yourself the three questions above to guide you to acceptance.

A bonus from this exercise once you master it is that you never need 'suffer' from feeling cold again, providing it's not too extended. You can feel the bite of a cold wind, just observing the feeling and accepting it.

The same applies to any other feeling.

WHAT WE RESIST WILL PERSIST

Some feelings such as fear, depression or anxiety can be perpetuated by our wishing they'd go away. Therefore, accepting these feelings can avoid unnecessarily perpetuating them. If we find ourselves feeling low or depressed and concentrate on how unpleasant it feels, worry about whether it will get worse or just wish we weren't feeling that way, we'll probably stay feeling low or depressed for a while.

But if we can accept that it's OK to feel that way for now and simply observe the feeling and fully experience it, it's likely to diminish a lot more quickly.

CASE STUDY

Gerry had a successful career, a good relationship, was comfortable with himself and his life, and was hopeful for the future.

He'd started practising pacceptance and through this had resolved some regrets and was now able to deal successfully with any issues that arose during the day.

Yet for some reason he had for a long time been experiencing periodic bouts of mild depression. He was still able to function fairly normally and eventually it would go away ... until the next time.

Gerry didn't know why he periodically felt depressed. There were no obvious events or thought patterns that seemed to trigger it. He was active and getting plenty of exercise, so a behavioural approach aimed at getting him more active wasn't open to us.

We could have spent a great deal of time delving into his past, his childhood and his unconscious thoughts to try to determine the source of the feeling. But I suggested we first try an acceptance approach.

On my suggestion, when he felt depressed he'd spend some time focusing on the feeling, making sure he was fully experiencing it and not avoiding it. He'd ask himself if the feeling was doing him any harm, which of course it wasn't, and whether he could bear it, which he certainly could.

Then he'd say to himself, with some conviction: 'It's perfectly OK to be experiencing this feeling for now and I completely accept it.' Gerry recounted later that the feeling seemed to diminish whenever he did this.

He repeated the exercise each day. Each time it seemed to diminish further and he thought it cleared up more quickly than previously.

He also noticed that each time he felt depressed it seemed less significant than before.

After a few times going through this exercise the depression stopped recurring and, as far as I'm aware, has never returned some years later.

Depression doesn't always respond so easily to a purely acceptance approach. Treatment is normally combined with behavioural change and, in some cases, challenging the thoughts behind the depression. Nevertheless accepting the feeling is generally a key aspect of an effective resolution.

By contrast, as we'll see:

Some uncomfortable feelings can immediately diminish and even completely disappear when we accept them.

For example, accepting that it's OK to feel fearful about something can immediately diminish the feeling. If we're anxious about speaking to an audience and we're worrying about how anxious we are or wishing we weren't feeling so anxious, we'll probably stay feeling anxious. But if we can accept that it's OK to feel anxious for now and that it's perfectly natural to feel that way, our anxiety will diminish a lot faster and may immediately disappear.

It doesn't work if we 'cheat'. If we accept a feeling in order to make it go away, we're not really accepting it. We need to be willing for it to remain for now. If it goes away as a result of accepting it (being willing for it to remain) then that's a bonus.

Anger or irritation can immediately diminish if we focus on it and accept the feeling. If someone cuts in front of you while you're driving, focusing on the feeling and accepting it should immediately clear up any irritation.

The reasons for this differ depending on the feeling. The most common source of anxiety is being anxious about being anxious, so accepting the feeling will usually diminish it as we're no longer so anxious about it. If we're feeling low or depressed we may simply be depressed about being depressed so accepting the feeling will diminish that aspect of our thinking.

When we accept anger or irritation, we're focusing on our feeling rather than whatever or whoever triggered it, so the negative thoughts that would otherwise reinforce the feeling are diminished.

Exercise

Next time you experience an uncomfortable feeling, focus on it, observe it and fully experience it. Instead of wishing it would go away, tell yourself that it's perfectly OK to have this feeling for now.

Try increasing the feeling. You won't succeed, but it will at least stop you trying to diminish it, avoid it or wish it would go away. You may be surprised by the result.

THE BEST WAY OUT IS THROUGH

Some feelings such as grief need time to work themselves through. Understanding that this is a natural process helps us to work through these feelings and at the same time can help to diminish the pain.

We may experience grief as a result of any loss. Losing someone we love through death or because they've left us, suffering a disability, losing our job, being robbed or experiencing any other significant loss can generate feelings of grief that just need time to resolve themselves.

Accepting these feelings, however, can help to diminish them and is likely to resolve them much more quickly.

SHARING OUR FEELINGS

Another benefit of accepting our feelings is that it makes it easier for us to communicate them to others. While there's usually no need to act on feelings such as anger (as we'll see in the next chapter), it doesn't do us any good to bottle them up.

Just talking about uncomfortable feelings can help to release the tension that may otherwise build up inside.

ACCEPT THE FEELING, CHOOSE THE ACTION

But by far the biggest benefit of accepting uncomfortable feelings is that it enables us to break the link between our feelings and our actions. It enables us to 'accept the feeling, choose the action'. This is the subject of the next chapter.

LETTING GO OF FEELINGS

When we've practised accepting uncomfortable feelings for a while, we can sometimes let them go. It's simply a case of deciding that we don't need the feeling any more and choosing to drop it. It isn't universally possible and the ability to do so varies between individuals, feelings and circumstances.

In my experience as a therapist, it's especially hard for people to let go of feelings before they've fully accepted them. If they do manage to, it's more likely they're suppressing the feeling so it will probably return.

The most important attribute remains being able to accept our uncomfortable feelings and any attempt to let them go shouldn't be at the expense of accepting them.

CASE STUDY

Godfrey had suffered from anxiety throughout the twenty years of his adult life. He became very anxious at the prospect of having to speak to a group and experienced symptoms such as a racing heart and shortness of breath.

Periodically he'd feel anxious without warning and as he worried where this might lead, the anxiety turned to mild panic (rapid acceleration of symptoms).

He'd always viewed his anxiety as uncontrollable and therefore frightening. The idea of accepting his feelings was new to him but he was persuaded to try it.

The next time he felt anxious he focused on the feeling and told himself it was perfectly OK and harmless. He adopted my suggestion of trying to make it worse, which immediately diminished it.

He quickly lost his fear of feeling anxious. For a while he still felt mildly anxious before speaking to groups, but this feeling had greatly diminished, dissipated quickly and no longer concerned him.

He no longer became anxious when under pressure and no longer experienced spontaneous anxiety or panic.

Then one day as he noticed himself becoming mildly anxious as usual before speaking to a group, he decided he just didn't need to any more. He chose to let the feeling go. He repeated this several more times, until it eventually stopped returning.

He now never becomes anxious and his confidence and abilities as a speaker have greatly improved.

So accepting uncomfortable feelings offers many benefits. It:

- Immediately reduces any dissatisfaction about whatever we're feeling
- Diminishes any feelings that may be perpetuated by wishing they'd go away and can make the feeling disappear altogether
- Helps us to work through feelings such as grief
- Makes it easier for us to communicate whatever we're feeling
- Enables us to break the link between feelings and actions (see Chapter 4)
- Allows us to let go of some uncomfortable feelings

These are significant benefits, making accepting our feelings one of the most valuable applications of accepting what is. In most situations, putting it into practice will have an immediate and dramatic impact on our lives. That's another **promise**.

Exercise

Start practising accepting any uncomfortable feelings all
the time. Try the shower exercise to get you started.

Every time you have an uncomfortable feeling, focus on
it, fully experience it and accept it, saying to yourself:
'It's OK to be experiencing this feeling for now.'

Make up your mind that you're going to accept any
uncomfortable feelings from now on. No exception. It's one
of the most powerful psychological tools you can learn and
practise.

Action summary

This chapter:

- Whenever you have an uncomfortable feeling, **fully experience and accept it**
- Try the **shower** exercise
- If an uncomfortable feeling keeps recurring when you've fully accepted it, **try letting it go**

Prior chapters:

- **Paccept** what is (our circumstances) at every opportunity
- Stop **worrying**
- **Observe** non-pacceptance in others (TV, etc.) and consider how you'd now think and act in their circumstances

CHAPTER 4

Breaking through

"Life is either a daring adventure or nothing." HELEN KELLER

Most people go through life allowing their feelings to determine their actions. If we're anxious, we tend to avoid whatever is making us anxious. If we're feeling low we tend to withdraw in some way. If we're feeling angry we tend to express it or retaliate.

This link between feelings and actions usually has an evolutionary purpose. Feelings evolved primarily for the purpose of getting us to take action. Feeling hungry drives us to eat. Feeling cold drives us to try to get warm. These feelings and responses are clearly helpful for our survival.

But our responses to feelings are not always so productive. Take anxiety for example. Anxiety originally evolved to encourage us to take action in response to rational fears, such as when faced with immediate danger. But these days most anxiety is experienced in response to less rational fears, such as phobias, social anxiety, fear of flying or public speaking.

Yet our response is still the same. We tend to avoid or move away from the source of anxiety. And this creates a problem that few people realise when they allow their feelings to determine their actions. Whenever we do what a feeling is telling us to do, we always reinforce the programming that's driving the feeling.

Feelings are always driven by a conscious or unconscious belief. If you had a dog phobia, the anxiety you would feel on seeing an approaching dog is driven by a conscious, or more likely unconscious, belief that dogs are threatening or dangerous. Perhaps this belief arose from you having been bitten by a dog when you were young.

That belief triggers anxiety when you see the dog. Most likely you would then avoid the dog, perhaps by crossing the road. You would do this for two reasons. First to avoid the dog, which you believe to be threatening or dangerous. Second to diminish your anxiety. But when you cross the road what would happen to your belief that dogs are dangerous? It would be reinforced.

Your avoidance sends a clear message to your unconscious mind: 'Dogs must be dangerous; otherwise why are we crossing the road?' A second reinforcement comes from the fact that when you cross the road your anxiety diminishes. This gives another message: 'Dogs must be dangerous; otherwise why would my anxiety diminish when I avoid the dog?'

This process is universal. Similar reinforcements occur whenever we do what any feeling is telling us to do. Depression is generally driven by a belief that life is in some way hopeless. People tend to withdraw or isolate themselves when depressed. This reinforces the belief that's driving the depression.

Anger is driven by a belief about injustice. When we're angry we tend to express our anger or retaliate in some way. This reinforces our belief that there's an injustice. The message received by our unconscious is: 'There must be an injustice; otherwise why would I be shouting or retaliating?' This isn't a problem for normal anger. But for someone with an 'anger problem' it will certainly reinforce the problem.

Cravings are driven by an unconscious belief that we need whatever we're craving. If we then consume whatever we're craving, we'll reinforce that belief. 'If I'm consuming the nicotine or chocolate, I must have needed it.'

Furthermore, in all these examples, whenever we do what a feeling is telling us to do, the feeling nearly always diminishes or goes away. As I explained with the dog phobia, this further reinforces the belief that's driving the feeling. 'If my chocolate craving goes away when I eat chocolate, then I must have needed chocolate.'

So the belief is strengthened in both ways and the feeling comes back stronger next time.

RESISTING FEELINGS

As we saw in the last chapter, as well as tending to do whatever our feelings are telling us to do, we also tend to 'resist' uncomfortable feelings. As we've seen, this has the effect of compounding the feelings. 'What we resist will persist.'

Resisting uncomfortable feelings also further encourages us to do whatever the feeling is telling us to do. When we cross the road to avoid the dog, our anxiety diminishes. When we eat the chocolate, our craving diminishes. So if we don't like what we're feeling, we'll cross the road or eat the chocolate to get rid of the feeling.

So resisting our uncomfortable feelings and then doing whatever the feelings are telling us to do is a perfect combination that is certain to compound the problem. Indeed, almost everyone who comes to see me with a psychological problem has developed that problem through a combination of resisting their uncomfortable feelings and repeatedly doing whatever those feelings have been telling them do.

THE CURE

It should now be clear what we need to do to resolve almost any psychological problem, unproductive habit or self-limitation, be it anxiety, depression, anger problems, OCD, addictions or any other self-limiting problem such as public speaking nerves, lack of confidence, low self-esteem, procrastination, smoking or excess weight.

First we need to train ourselves to accept any uncomfortable feelings. Then we need to repeatedly do the opposite of whatever the feeling is telling us to do. We need to:

Accept the feeling, choose the action.

This is probably the most powerful psychological tool anyone can develop in their lifetime. Learning to accept uncomfortable feelings was covered in the last chapter. Choosing an action that's opposite to whatever the feeling is telling us is something anyone can do, provided they're sufficiently motivated. The motivation is that it will resolve their problem or self-limitation, whatever that might be.

When we choose an action opposite to whatever the feeling is telling us to do, we undermine the belief that's driving the feeling. When we stop crossing the road and instead walk past the dog, our unconscious belief is immediately challenged. Our unconscious thinks, 'I thought dogs were dangerous, so why aren't we crossing the road? Maybe dogs aren't dangerous after all.' Doing this repeatedly, while accepting the anxiety, or any other recurring feeling, will eventually eliminate the feeling.

Furthermore, because I'm accepting my anxiety, it's easier to walk past the dog as I no longer need to cross the road to avoid feeling anxious.

Finally if I'm controlling my anxiety by accepting it, the challenge to my belief that dogs are dangerous is strengthened. My unconscious thinks: 'If I'm not feeling so anxious maybe there's no danger.' And so my belief about dogs unwinds all the faster.

ACCEPT THE FEELING, CHOOSE THE ACTION

We have a lot more immediate control over our actions than we have over our feelings. So we can choose to act in productive ways, whatever we're feeling. We can:

> *Accept the feeling, choose the action.*

This isn't just a glib phrase. It's a life-changing tool for dealing with recurring uncomfortable feelings and unproductive habits, breaking through limitations and taking charge in challenging situations.

It's a way of thinking and acting that allows us to separate our feelings from our actions. Living our lives according to this adage allows us to act in ways that are no longer determined by our feelings. And if we want to resolve feelings such as anxiety, reticence, feeling low, addiction, excessive desire for food or an anger problem, we need to repeatedly accept the feeling (or desire) and then act in a way that's opposite to whatever the feeling is telling us to do.

If we're feeling low and we want to resolve the feeling, we need to 'accept the feeling, choose the action'. We need to accept the low feeling and re-engage with life, such as responding positively to social invitations, getting more exercise, developing a passionate interest or contributing to others.

CASE STUDY

Mary had been depressed for years. It turned out that the initial source of her depression was an unwanted teenage pregnancy. Her parents had persuaded her to give up her child for adoption.

Her ensuing regret, self-blame, low esteem and consequent depression had resulted in her avoiding forming any lasting relationship.

In the next chapter I'll explain how we resolved her self-blame. To resolve her depression fully she also needed to 'accept the feeling, choose the action'.

During the years when she'd felt depressed, she'd continued to live with her parents, had socialised little and kept to herself, even going home from work at lunchtimes rather than lunching with her workmates.

At my suggestion she began taking regular aerobic exercise, started to mix more with her workmates, both at lunchtimes and when opportunities arose in the evenings, and took up dancing as a hobby and as a boost to her exercise programme. She moved out of home and into shared accommodation. At weekends she volunteered to help out with a charity that organised outings for disabled children. All this despite feeling depressed.

To ensure she was accepting and not resisting her feelings, she spent a few minutes each day sitting quietly and focusing on her feelings, telling herself they were harmless and perfectly OK to be experiencing for now. (This practice is known as 'Mindfulness'.)

Her depression soon lifted and shortly after she found herself in the relationship she'd been avoiding for years.

More severe problems, such as major or clinical depression, need other tools in addition to this one. One of these is a 'cognitive restructuring' technique called a thought record (outlined in Chapter 10, 'Our crazy thoughts'). This is a Cognitive-Behavioural Therapy (CBT) technique that aims to directly challenge distorted ways of thinking. But for most issues, accepting our uncomfortable feelings and choosing productive actions is the best way to challenge the unconscious beliefs that are driving our feelings and behaviour.

For example, if we have a problem with excessive anger, our anger is likely to result in us responding excessively to perceived injustices. If we want to resolve the problem we need to repeatedly accept the feeling and withhold the angry response.

CASE STUDY

David had an anger problem that was affecting his work and family life. One particular flare-up at work led to him being referred to me for help.

We quickly determined that the issue had originated with an injustice he experienced when he was very young. Knowing this provided some help with his self-esteem. But this didn't immediately resolve his anger.

He also needed to learn to 'accept the feeling, choose the action'.

David practised accepting his feelings, first with the shower exercise and then transferring this learning to his anger. He agreed to experiment with holding back on any angry response while he focused on, and accepted, his feelings.

He also learned to own his reactions, which we'll cover in the chapter called 'It's all about me' (see Chapter 9).

His anger 'problem' was effectively resolved, at least from everyone else's perspective, as soon as he took control of his angry responses. But his angry reactions (feelings) also started to diminish as soon as he changed his behaviour and after a while were fully resolved.

Choosing our actions may mean choosing to defer a current gratification for the sake of a longer-term benefit. I may feel a strong desire to tuck into that cream cake but I can accept the desire and choose not to indulge it if I want to lose weight. The excessive desire to eat beyond what we need will gradually unwind.

I may be experiencing cravings for nicotine, sugar or chocolate. If I can repeatedly accept the craving and choose not to indulge it, the craving will gradually diminish and eventually disappear.

> *Self-discipline and self-control starts*
> *with recognising we have the power*
> *to choose our actions whatever*
> *we may be feeling.*

It doesn't require us to suppress our feelings or desires, and it generally doesn't help to try to. We don't need to deal with the feeling, beyond accepting it. Nor do we need to wait for it to subside to choose a productive action that's not determined by whatever we're feeling.

CASE STUDY

Tara had been struggling with a weight problem for years. When I met her, it became clear she used eating to cover up uncomfortable feelings. If she felt anxious or low, she'd eat, giving her a sense of having control over her feelings.

The idea of fully experiencing and accepting her feelings was initially scary for her. I persuaded her to experiment with the shower exercise described in the previous chapter. Once she'd mastered this, she was willing to apply the same 'acceptance' approach to other feelings.

She found that accepting her feelings diminished them as much as, and usually more than, eating. Even when her feelings didn't immediately diminish through acceptance, she was no longer fearful of them.

Having learned to accept her feelings, Tara was able to apply the adage 'accept the feeling, choose the action' to her eating. She was able to accept her feelings and choose not to eat, except lightly at mealtimes.

The kilos began to fall off her.

BREAKING THROUGH FEAR

Fear in its various forms can limit us more than any other feeling if we let it. Insecurity and fear of failure are perfectly normal feelings given the way we've learned to think and react. But they don't have to stop us doing the things we want to do if we choose not to let them.

I'm talking here about irrational fears – situations we can see aren't dangerous to our health or safety and aren't unreasonably risky, but that we feel nervous or reticent about because of our unconscious programming and automatic ways of thinking.

I may need to talk to a group but feel anxious about speaking in front of audiences. I may want to raise an issue with my boss, but feel self-conscious about doing so.

The way through is to:

Accept the feeling, choose the action.

We can hold the fear in one hand while we do what we want to do with the other. We don't have to wait until our fear has subsided. If first-time parachutists waited for the fear to subside before jumping, the plane would be up there for a very long time.

One of the reasons we're so reluctant to act when we feel fearful is that we have a belief, either conscious or unconscious, that if we do it something disastrous may happen.

The best way to challenge this belief is to do whatever we're afraid of while accepting the fear, and thus prove to ourselves, and to our unconscious mind, that it doesn't lead to disaster.

So when we're faced with something we're afraid of, instead of seeing our fear as an obstacle that has to be overcome, we can see it as an opportunity to deal with the very programming that's causing us to feel afraid.

The way to change the programming is to start doing the things we're fearful or reticent about and to keep doing them, until we get the message that we don't need to be fearful any more.

When we practise 'accept the feeling, choose the action', we may discover we have a lot more potential than we realised. As our fears or reticence start to diminish, and we're no longer so limited by them, it becomes easier to choose productive actions, both day to day and longer term.

CASE STUDY

Lucy suffered from social anxiety. She'd turn down social invitations for fear of not being able to handle the inevitable interactions and making a fool of herself.

She had the idea that one day the anxiety would go away and she'd be able to be more social. I explained she was an unwitting victim of the 'when-then syndrome': 'When my anxiety goes away, then I'll ....' Lucy needed to start by accepting her feelings of anxiety while she did the very thing she was afraid of.

She began by inviting a neighbour to coffee, holding onto her fear in one hand while she took action with the other. She made it easier by being open with her neighbour and explaining what she was doing.

Very soon she was taking on bigger challenges. Her social anxiety was quickly resolved.

In all areas of our lives, choosing our actions means dealing with problems or issues instead of trying to avoid them.

There may be a problem at work that we're not sure how to handle. Avoiding it and hoping it will go away usually doesn't help. Talking it through with others, seeking advice, making a start and tackling it one step at a time are all more productive.

If we feel nervous or reticent about asserting ourselves or tackling a problem, that's fine. We can just hold on to, and accept, our nervousness or reticence and choose to do whatever needs to be done.

Exercise

Is there any area of your life where you're being held back by fear or reticence? Is there something you'd do if you had no fear that you're not doing?

Resolve to accept the feeling while you do whatever it is you would have done if you had no fear.

Set a date by which you'll take the action. Then do it. If it's too big a step to take in one go, set a smaller goal and a date by which you'll take that action. When you've done it, increase the challenge.

If you think you can't do it because it's too fearful, the answer is, yes you absolutely can, even if you have to attack it one step at a time. See it as an opportunity. The bigger the challenge, the bigger the impact will be on your life when you break through the fear.

PRACTISING

Rather than just applying this tool to specific issues we may want to resolve, it pays to practise it in any area of our lives where unproductive behaviour is being driven by an aversion to discomfort.

For example, most people are aware that exercise is good for our health, fitness and physique. Yet many people miss daily opportunities to exercise simply because it can initially generate discomfort. Taking every opportunity to exercise, such as walking up two flights of stairs instead of taking the lift, walking quickly instead of at our normal pace, walking up escalators or getting off the bus a stop earlier are not only opportunities to exercise and get fitter, they're also opportunities to practise 'accept the feeling, choose the action'.

Exercise may initially generate muscle discomfort or more rapid breathing. We can focus on those feelings and accept them, knowing they won't harm us and that they're bearable. Then we can choose to keep up the exercise.

If we start living our lives by the principle of 'accept the feeling, choose the action', we can start doing things we previously might have seen as beyond our reach. As our lives expand, the possibilities also expand. That's my latest **promise** to you. There's no limit to what we might achieve if we keep it up, taking on new challenges and repeatedly moving beyond our comfort zone.

Action summary

This chapter:

- **'Accept the feeling, choose the action'** to resolve recurring uncomfortable feelings, unproductive habits and self-limitations
- Use it to **take action** even when fearful
- **Practise**

Prior chapters:

- 'Accept for now' any uncomfortable **feelings** (fully experience and accept them)
- **Paccept** what is (our circumstances) at every opportunity
- Stop **worrying**
- If an uncomfortable feeling keeps recurring when you've fully accepted it, **try letting it go**
- **Observe** non-pacceptance in others (TV, etc.) and consider how you'd now think and act in their circumstances

Note that accepting feelings is now at the top of the list. That's because if we have an emotional reaction, we normally need to deal with it first, by focusing on and accepting the feeling, which will usually diminish it, before we can paccept the circumstances that triggered the feeling.

CHAPTER 5

An extraordinary truth

"To regret one's experience is to deny one's existence."
OSCAR WILDE

I'm about to introduce you to an extraordinary truth about life, so make yourself comfortable, relax, take a deep breath and be prepared for a surprise.

I'm going to challenge the way you've probably always thought about a great many things. Some of you will initially resist this challenge. You may at first think, as I did, that what I'm going to tell you can't be true. Perhaps you'll think you now have the evidence to get your own back. You'll think I'm the one who's crazy.

Since the benefits of understanding and using this truth are so great I'll do my best, as I always have, to convince you.

THE EASY BIT

The way we think, feel and act in a particular situation is determined by three things:

1 Our attitudes or ways of thinking, including our beliefs

2 Our personality, which in this book means our unconscious programming

3 Our abilities, including our knowledge

There's also our mood or 'state of mind', which can vary from day to day or moment to moment. But our mood is determined by the interaction between our recent circumstances and our attitudes, personality and abilities so these three are still the prime determinants.

- A man whose attitudes include the belief that men don't cook is unlikely to want to sign up for a cooking course
- Those of us whose personality (unconscious programming) includes a fear of heights would feel pretty uncomfortable perched on a ledge several storeys up
- Someone who has strong abilities as a tennis player is likely to play a better game of tennis than someone who hasn't

So far, there's nothing surprising about any of this.

Our attitudes, personality and abilities overlap and influence each other. So in practice our thoughts, feelings and actions result from a complex interaction between our attitudes, personality and abilities, together with our mood and circumstances at the time.

LIFE HISTORY

What determines our attitudes, personality and abilities? They're the cumulative result of all our past experiences, including our conscious and unconscious thoughts, the choices we've made along the way and our genetic or inherited traits. We call all this our life history.

The man who believes that men don't cook probably developed his belief as a result of past experiences, including perhaps the views of at least one of his parents and his past conscious or unconscious thoughts based on the things he's seen or heard.

Those of us who have a fear of heights probably acquired it as a result of childhood experiences, together with the unconscious thoughts that resulted from those experiences and perhaps some inherited traits.

Our abilities as a tennis player depend on how often we've played, how motivated we were at the time and our coordination skills, which may in turn have been determined by childhood experiences and inherited traits.

The development of our attitudes, personality and abilities continues throughout our lives as a result of new thoughts and experiences. Your attitudes or beliefs now are hopefully slightly different from an hour ago or from a time before you started reading this book.

> *The way we think, feel and act in a particular situation is determined by who we are at that moment (attitudes, personality and abilities), which is in turn determined by our life history up to that moment.*

If this is so why are we often disappointed by our thoughts, feelings or actions or think they should have been different?

If through nervousness or lack of ability or poor preparation I've performed badly in a job interview, why might I be annoyed or disappointed with myself? Clearly if I am, it's because my performance fell short of my hopes or expectations.

But what I did was determined by my attitudes, personality and abilities at the time, which in turn were determined by my life history up to that moment. So wasn't I just doing my best given my attitudes, etc., and my mood and circumstances at the time? In other words, given my life history up to that moment?

If I'd known how to do better or how not to be nervous or had the foresight to be more prepared, I'd have done it. But I didn't know. So I was being the best I knew how to be at that moment.

MAKING CHOICES

You might agree in my example that I may not have known how to control my nervousness or do anything about my lack of ability, at least at the time, but surely I had a choice about my degree of preparation. So isn't it reasonable to think poorly of myself or be disappointed with myself for not being more prepared?

What if I went out socialising with my friends the night before rather than prepare for the interview?

Well, here's the surprise I promised you. When I chose to go out with my friends, I was doing my best given my attitudes or ways of thinking at the time. And those attitudes were determined by my life history up to that moment. In fact:

> *We've always been doing our best at any moment, given our attitudes, personality and abilities at the time and hence given our life history up to that moment.*

The question is not whether we make choices, because we surely do. The question is: why do we make the choices we make? The answer is always because of who we are (attitudes, personality, abilities) at that moment, which in turn is determined by our life history up to that moment.

Why do two people make a different choice in the same circumstances? Because they have different attitudes, etc. as a result of different life histories up to that moment.

Why does the same person make a different choice at different times in the same circumstances? Because their attitudes, or perhaps their resulting mood, are different at those different times, which in turn can only be explained by their recent experiences up to the moment when they made the different choice.

Why are some of you feeling a little uncomfortable with the suggestion that we've always been doing our best, given our attitudes, etc. at the time, while others are perfectly happy with the idea? Because we all have different attitudes, etc. as a result of our different life histories.

You may be thinking the idea that we've always been doing our best, given our attitudes, etc. at the time sounds like a cop-out. You may already be thinking about issues such as responsibility, accountability, cruelty, selfishness and crime. We'll deal with all of these.

Hopefully what I'm going to tell you, which by the time we've finished will form part of your life history, will be sufficient to make you all comfortable, irrespective of what you may be thinking right now. For example, I'll be saying:

> *We're absolutely still responsible for our actions.*

I'll also be saying that understanding we've always been doing our best, given who we were at the time, only has value if at the same time we take responsibility for our past, present and future actions, particularly if we've hurt or harmed others by our actions.

FREE WILL

Free will is the ability to make choices that aren't determined by our history. There's a school of philosophy called determinism, which claims everything that happens is determined by everything that's happened before. In determinist philosophy there's no such thing as free will.

Modern science, specifically the science of quantum mechanics, provides evidence to suggest that random or at least unpredictable events are occurring all the time. This means those events aren't determined by what's happened before. Perhaps our intuitive thoughts are to some extent random or unpredictable.

This suggests the future couldn't be predicted even if we had a complete understanding of how the human mind works. But this still leaves open the question of whether we have free will.

There are some who believe the human mind ceases to be determined when we're connected to our spiritual or higher self. This suggests we can freely choose to move towards a higher purpose but, when we choose otherwise, our thoughts, feelings and actions are determined by our history.

We won't be exploring spiritual ideas in this book. This is a subject for another time. But it doesn't change the notion that we've always been doing our best at any moment, given who we are at the time.

When I first stumbled on this idea I realised how powerful it could be in the context of pacceptance. At first I found it hard to believe. So I consulted academics in the fields of philosophy, psychology and neuro-science who all told me the idea I'd stumbled on was undoubtedly true.

Since then I've yet to meet a philosopher, psychologist or neuro-scientist with an understanding of the subject who believes otherwise. In other words:

> *All those who understand the subject of determinism and free will believe the human mind is determined. This means the choices we make in any given circumstances are determined by who we are at that moment, which in turn is determined by our life history up to that moment.*

You can search for Bertrand Russell or Albert Einstein on the internet together with the word 'determinism' and see for yourself.

So when I chose to go out with my friends instead of preparing for my interview, that choice was determined by who I was at that moment (attitudes, personality and abilities), together with my mood and circumstances, which was in turn determined by my life history up to that moment.

I've met few people who realise the practical significance of this truth as relatively few are familiar with the concept of 'accepting what is' and most have never heard of pacceptance. You may already be able to see the significance in the context of pacceptance. In short, subject to what I'm going to say about responsibility, it can eliminate regret and self-blame from our lives. I'll explain this shortly.

Here's the ultimate argument about free will. Even if free will does play a role in the choices we make, it seems reasonable to suppose we'd use it as best we can to satisfy our needs or wants or our perception of other people's needs or wants, at the time. And those needs, wants and perceptions are themselves determined by our attitudes, personality and abilities at the time.

So we still come back to these three as being the determinants of what we think, feel and do, together with our mood and circumstances, and these three determinants can only be a product of our life history up to this moment.

From now on, for the sake of brevity, I'll summarise the phrase 'attitudes, personality and abilities' with the word 'awareness'. In our language, this word usually means what we're focusing on or conscious of. For the purpose of this book, I've borrowed the word and expanded its meaning to include everything that makes us who we are at the moment.

DOING OUR BEST OR DOING THE ONLY THING WE COULD HAVE DONE?

I'm saying we've always been doing our best at any moment given our awareness at the time. The truth is:

> *We've always done the only thing we could have done at any moment, given our awareness at the time.*

For us to have done something different we'd have needed a different awareness at that moment. And in order to have a different awareness we'd have needed a different life history up to that moment, however small that difference might be.

When I chose to go out with my friends the evening before my interview, that was the only choice I could have made at that moment, given my awareness at the time, and hence given my life history up to that moment.

I'll mainly use the expression 'we've always done our best at any moment, given our awareness at the time' but if you prefer you could replace it with 'we've always done the only thing we could have done at any moment, given our awareness at the time'.

Most of the time I'll mention both as I've found that some prefer the more positive sounding version (doing our best) and others the more accurate version (the only thing we could have done). Both are true.

CASE STUDY

Nelson had a successful career in a large multinational company. He'd risen rapidly and adapted well to the increasing responsibility that came with each promotion ... until a month before I met him.

He'd taken his eye off the ball and made a costly mistake. The setback, for which he blamed himself entirely, and the resulting negative feedback from senior management had unnerved him and damaged his confidence.

When I explained to him that he'd always done his best with the awareness he had at the time and that the mistake he'd made was the only thing he could have done at that moment, he was able to let go of his regret and self-blame.

He understood he was still responsible. We'll come back to this case when we look at the difference between responsibility and self-blame later in this chapter.

EXPECTATIONS

It's good to have high expectations of ourselves. In fact, high expectations usually have a beneficial effect on our performance. But when our performance doesn't match our expectations, is there any reason to think we 'should' have done better, if in fact we were doing our best (the only thing we could have done) given our awareness at the time?

If we had perfect foresight through a complete understanding of how we'd behave at a particular moment in a particular situation, our expectations would always match our performance. We don't have this foresight and life might be rather dull if we did, but does this give us reason to think it was our expectations that were right while our performance was somehow wrong?

It's not that we couldn't have done better given our abilities. But something would have had to be different. If I'd been more positive about my interview or better prepared or less worried about the outcome, I may well have done better. But this would have meant being a different person at that moment with a different awareness, which in turn would have required a different life history up to that moment.

> *If the experience helps me to realise how I could have done better, my life history and awareness have now changed and I can do better next time.*

THE UNHELPFUL 'SHOULD'

Even if we didn't have any particular hopes or expectations about something we did, the same argument still applies. Looking back at the things we've done, is there any reason to think we should have done better?

Telling ourselves we should have done something different makes sense if we're just pointing out where we went wrong or what we'd need to have done differently in order to get a better result. Thinking about this will help us do better next time.

But it makes little sense if we use the word 'should' in a regretful, self-blaming way if we were doing our best (the only thing we could have done) given who we were at that moment.

CASE STUDY

I described Mary in the last chapter. You may recall she'd been depressed for several years. The initial source of her depression was an unwanted teenage pregnancy. Her parents had persuaded her to give up her child for adoption.

Over the ensuing years she'd developed a sense of loss fuelled by regret and self-blame around becoming pregnant and giving up her child and a belief that she'd been an 'inadequate mother'.

Her regret, self-blame, low esteem and consequent depression had resulted in her avoiding forming any lasting relationship.

When Mary learned that she'd always been doing her best (the only thing she could have done) given her awareness at the time and hence given her life history up to each moment, her sense of regret and self-blame dissolved.

Her depression soon lifted with the help of 'accepting her feelings and choosing her actions' as described in the last chapter.

WE'RE STILL RESPONSIBLE

You may be concerned that this way of thinking seems like a cop-out. But eliminating regret and self-blame doesn't mean diminishing our responsibility.

> *We alone control our actions, we alone can choose them and we alone have the power, and can use that power, to act responsibly now and in the future.*

We chose the actions we took and will continue to choose the actions we take in future. We are and always will be responsible for our actions. No one else can take that responsibility away from us except perhaps when we were very young. Far from diminishing our sense of responsibility we'll be talking about the importance of developing it.

But we need to recognise that the value of acknowledging our responsibility for past events lies only in the influence this has on the future. After all, what's done is done and cannot be changed. And we now know it couldn't have been different. But if I've behaved irresponsibly in the past and, being aware of this, I choose to continue to behave this way in the future then I believe this is indeed a cop-out and for me the principle of doing my best ceases to have any value.

If we take responsibility for our past actions but at the same time understand we were doing our best (the only thing we could have done) with the awareness we had at the time, we can stop blaming ourselves and focus instead on what we need to do to make amends and change the way we behave in the future.

> *Self-blame involves thinking our past actions should have been different, which is a nonsense because they couldn't have been different, given our awareness at the time. Taking responsibility for our past actions focuses on what we need to do differently now and in the future, such as making amends or changing our behaviour.*

Self-blame involves statements or thoughts such as:

- 'I should/shouldn't have …' (in a regretful/self-blaming way)
- 'If only I had/hadn't …'

Such thoughts have no value, are unproductive and above all make no sense, first because we cannot undo the past and second because we were doing our best (the only thing we could have done) given our awareness at the time.

Taking responsibility, on the other hand, involves statements or thoughts such as:

■ 'What I did was wrong or ineffective so I need to act differently in future'

■ 'I'm responsible for what I did so what can I do to make amends, such as apologise, commit to behave differently in future or accept whatever penalties or other consequences result from the actions I took?'

Such thoughts are valuable, productive and, unlike self-blame, make sense.

> *If we're using the principle of doing our best to eliminate regret and self-blame we also need to take responsibility for what we did and, where applicable, commit to change our behaviour in the future and make amends for the past.*

CASE STUDY

You'll recall from earlier in this chapter that when Nelson understood his costly mistake was the only thing he could have done with the awareness he had at the time, he let go of regret and self-blame.

He was still responsible for what happened. But he could now see that the value of recognising that responsibility lay only in how it impacted his attitudes and behaviour now and in the future, such as taking action to ensure it couldn't happen again.

Since Nelson was a capable contributor in his work environment, taking responsibility sat a lot more easily with him than blaming himself for the past. His sense of self-worth was restored and he once again became highly motivated.

Given that our actions were determined by our awareness at the time, are we not responsible for the way our awareness has developed? Yes we are. No one else can take that responsibility away from us, again except perhaps when we were very young.

But blaming ourselves for our faults and weaknesses implies we chose them. The fact is we don't consciously choose our characteristics. They develop as a consequence of our thoughts and experiences and the choices we make along the way.

There's no sense putting ourselves down because of the past thoughts, feelings and actions that have determined how our awareness developed, if again we were only doing our best (the only thing we could have done) at each moment.

Once again, the value of taking responsibility for how our awareness developed lies in what we choose to do now and in the future to change it, to avoid repeating past mistakes and, where appropriate, make amends.

CASE STUDY

Nicola had a major regret about not having continued her education beyond school. She'd chosen instead to work to earn money to fund her social life and an expensive hobby. Soon after this decision she married and started a family. When I met her she felt she'd missed her chance of developing a fulfilling career.

When Nicola learned and understood that the decision not to continue her education was the only decision she could have taken with the awareness she had at the time, she was able to let go of her regret.

She was still responsible for her decision but the value of recognising this lay only in the impact it had on her current and future decisions.

Having let go of regret and self-blame she was now able to take greater control of her life. She enrolled in an Open University degree and later obtained the qualification needed to launch herself on her chosen career.

NOT NECESSARILY OUR BEST EFFORT OR BEST USE OF OUR ABILITIES

If I think I've:

■ Made a bad choice

■ Made a mess of a relationship

■ Missed an opportunity because I was lacking in confidence

■ Had an accident through carelessness

I was doing my best (the only thing I could have done) given my awareness at the time. So there's no reason to chastise myself or feel disappointed with myself. Rather I can learn from the experience and resolve to do better next time.

Doing our best doesn't necessarily mean making our greatest effort or doing things to the best of our ability. It may just mean doing whatever we believe appropriate to satisfy our needs or wants or the needs or wants of others at the time.

And one person's idea of the best or most appropriate thing to do may be quite different from another's. This again depends on our attitudes at the time.

But we were doing our best given our abilities and attitudes at that moment and those attitudes were determined by our life history up to that moment.

If we have conflicting needs or wants we'll tend to favour the one that seems most significant at the time. If I think I ought to be painting the house but I'm feeling lazy, I may choose to watch TV. Looking back I was doing my best in the light of my conflicting needs or wants and my attitudes, however unproductive, at that moment.

AND SO TO PACCEPTANCE

Understanding we were doing our best or doing the only thing we could have done, given our awareness at the time, is a powerful alternative justification for paccepting our past actions.

> *We can paccept the things we've done or haven't done not just because there's no point wishing things were already different but also because we were doing our best (the only thing we could have done) at that moment, given our awareness at the time.*

So we can avoid perpetuating any regret, disappointment or self-blame we may experience when our actions fall short of our expectations.

The pacceptance process introduced in Chapter 1 now becomes:

- Notice whenever we're regretting or blaming ourselves for something we've just done, or did or didn't do a while ago
- Understand we were doing our best (the only thing we could have done) given our awareness at the time
- Drop the regret or self-blaming thought
- Refocus on what we can do, if anything, to improve the future, such as rectifying the situation, making amends or taking action to ensure it doesn't happen again

CASE STUDY

Stephen was addicted to drugs. He'd been through rehab several times and each time had relapsed. His parents had paid a great deal for these failed attempts.

When I met him his self-esteem was low. He felt worthless and a failure. His failed attempts to come off drugs also had a lot to do with his anger towards his parents.

There was a great deal we needed to work through to resolve his anger and give him the strength to beat his addiction. The tools we used are outlined in this book.

But before he could forgive his parents for whatever he blamed them for and build his own sense of power we needed to deal with his low self-esteem. His breakthrough began with learning that at every moment in his challenging life he'd done his best (the only thing he could have done) with the awareness he had at the time.

No one had explained this to Stephen before. As with most of my clients who hear it for the first time I can recall the look on his face as he took it in and realised both the truth and the power of what he was hearing.

Even before I mentioned it, he understood the implications not only to his own sense of regret and self-worth but also to his attitude towards his parents (we'll cover this later).

He let go of his regret and self-blame around his past behaviour. He quickly understood the difference between self-blame and responsibility and that responsibility was only relevant to the choices he made from now on.

He began taking responsibility for his past and future actions. From that moment Stephen's self-esteem began to rise and his attitudes began to change. We'll follow his case through several chapters of this book.

IMPROVING THE FUTURE

Understanding we were doing our best (the only thing we could have done) at any moment, given our awareness at the time, helps us to recognise that something has to change in our awareness if we want to do better next time. Sometimes this happens automatically as a result of experience. But it's more likely to happen if we recognise we need to make a conscious decision to change.

CASE STUDY

The first time I forgot to turn off my mobile phone in a meeting was also the last time it happened (with one or two exceptions in one-to-one meetings in around ten years). I was presenting to a large meeting at the time and it was an important one.

When it rang to my initial embarrassment, in the few seconds it took me to turn it off I accepted my initial feeling of embarrassment, paccepted what had happened (I immediately knew that when I left it on I'd been doing my best given my awareness at the time, so I couldn't possibly have turned it off on that occasion) and resolved that every time I walked into a meeting from then on, I'd turn it off.

That resolution was the change in awareness that resulted in my not leaving it on again. Without that resolution it would probably have happened again and again until I finally got the message and resolved to change my behaviour or until I learned automatically from the repeated negative experience and developed a habit of turning it off.

As we discussed in the first chapter, pacceptance removes dissatisfaction and empowers us to make changes to improve the future. We now have a more powerful justification for pacceptance whenever self-blame is involved and an effective tool for enabling us to focus on what we need to do to change what we do in the future.

ELIMINATING GUILT

As well as there being no place for regret once we've mastered pacceptance, particularly if we resolve to learn from our mistakes and take responsibility for our actions, there's also no reason to feel guilty about something we've done that's unintentionally hurt others.

If we've unwittingly let others down or hurt them when we were only doing our best (the only thing we could have done), we should acknowledge our responsibility but there's no need to blame ourselves.

If we had good intentions but were lacking in ability or awareness at the time we can resolve to do better in future. But there's no point hitting ourselves over the head for our past unintentional errors.

CASE STUDY

Jo had a good job and a loving family. But for the past several years he'd suffered constant regret and guilt about a bad investment that had lost a great deal of money. He felt guilty because of the significant impact on his family's standard of living.

He felt doubly bad because he'd been advised by a friend not to go ahead and had instead listened to others who he knew had something to gain from his making the investment.

He learned about pacceptance as I've described in Chapter 1. This helped but didn't immediately eliminate his regret and guilt. He still felt he 'shouldn't' have done what he did and so blamed himself.

Then he learned that when he made the investment he was doing his best with the awareness he had at that time. Indeed making the investment was the only thing he could possibly have done with the awareness he had at that moment. And the awareness he had was determined by his life history up to that time, including all the advice he'd received.

Jo was now able to fully paccept what had happened. He naturally still would have 'preferred' it hadn't happened but now that he understood there was no way it couldn't have happened his regret and guilt were completely resolved.

He still acknowledged responsibility for his past actions, but understood this was only relevant to the choices he made from now on.

WHAT IF WE'VE KNOWINGLY HURT OTHERS?

What if we've knowingly behaved in a cruel, unduly selfish, hurtful or otherwise unfair way towards others? First, as always, we need to take responsibility (acknowledge our past errors, make amends wherever we can and resolve not to act this way again).

Second, it's reasonable to feel remorse for past actions that we knew to be unfair at the time. But if we take responsibility for what we've done we can forgive ourselves or ask others for forgiveness and so work through any remorse we may justifiably be feeling.

Understanding that we've always been doing our best is no excuse for continuing to behave in unduly selfish, inconsiderate or hurtful ways in the future. On the contrary, letting go of self-blame and recognising that our past actions were determined by our awareness at the time gives us a better chance to change our attitudes and behaviour in the future if we've been behaving inappropriately in the past.

> *If we're not prepared to take responsibility and change our attitudes and behaviour in the future then the principle of doing our best has no value.*

PAST NOT PRESENT

Applying the principle of doing our best to our thoughts and actions only works in the past not the present. I'd never say to myself: 'I'm being irresponsible, selfish or inconsiderate right now but I'm only doing my best with the awareness I have at this moment.' Such a thought would be misleading, unhelpful and unproductive.

If we try to apply the principle to our attitudes or actions in the present it's no longer valid since, as soon as we say it or think it, our awareness immediately changes.

As soon as I say to myself, 'I'm being selfish right now,' I can choose to stop being selfish if I want to.

By contrast it can be useful to apply it to our feelings in the present since these are not usually within our immediate control. It would be perfectly reasonable to say or think, 'I'm feeling anxious and that's the only thing I could be feeling with the awareness I have right now.'

CAN IT REALLY BE TRUE?

The idea that we've always been doing our best, or the only thing we could have done, at every moment will for most be an unfamiliar concept.

We've been told or told ourselves so often that we could and should have done better, that the suggestion 'we've always done our best' or 'the only thing we could have done' may have raised a few doubts or questions, let alone eyebrows.

What if looking back on something we've done, we can see how we could have done better? Were we then doing our best?

If we'd been aware of how to do better at the time we'd have done it so we were doing our best with the knowledge and insights we had then. Is it reasonable to chastise ourselves or be disappointed with ourselves for not having had greater insight at the time? I don't believe so.

We might have more insight now because the circumstances are different – more experience, more time to think, etc. Why should we have had that insight then?

CASE STUDY

Sonia blamed herself for the break-up of her marriage. She had constantly pressured her husband into being somebody he wasn't. When she married she'd harboured expectations about a lifestyle that her husband simply couldn't meet.

Now that she'd had time to reflect, she realised how unfair she'd been and felt a strong sense of guilt about how she'd behaved. She knew he'd adored her and had tried to meet her expectations. She now believed that if she hadn't been so demanding, their marriage could have been a success.

When she learned that she'd always been doing her best, given her awareness at the time, and that indeed she'd always done the only thing she could have done given that awareness, she was able to let go of her regret, guilt and self-blame.

She understood she was still responsible but that this only impacted her choices about the future.

Both she and her husband had moved on by the time I met Sonia. But she at least felt she could benefit from her new awareness, not just by letting go of her regret and self-blame, but also in choosing different ways to behave in her current relationship.

If we've had an argument with someone and think we should have avoided it or handled it better, why should we? We handled it as well as we were able to with our awareness at the time. But we can learn from the experience and choose to act differently in future.

What if we've made a mess of something because we didn't make enough effort?

Quite probably we considered at the time that the effort we were making was sufficient. Or we were prepared to take a risk that it might not be. If, with the benefit of hindsight, we now know we were mistaken, we were still doing what we considered appropriate at the time.

Again, we can learn from the experience and choose to make more effort next time.

Exercise

Think about something you've done, or haven't done, that you regret. See if you can identify the attitudes, unconscious programming or abilities that influenced your actions at the time. (We don't normally need to do this … it's just for this exercise.)

Acknowledge that you were only doing whatever seemed appropriate, or whatever you were able to do, with the awareness you had at that moment. See it as part of the process by which we learn and become wiser.

Choose to paccept your past action or inaction on the grounds that you did the only thing you could have done with the awareness you had at the time. Let go of any regret. If appropriate, resolve to act differently in future.

What if we've behaved in a self-destructive way, such as abusing alcohol or drugs or over-eating when we want to lose weight?

We may not have been aware at the time of the consequences of our behaviour, or the benefits of changing it. If we were aware that we were behaving in a self-destructive way, we may not have had the motivation or the ability to change our behaviour at that time.

Perhaps we weren't aware we had the power, and could harness that power, to make a more productive choice. If we'd had that motivation, ability and awareness, we'd have stopped then.

CASE STUDY

When Stephen learned that his slide into drug taking, and the relapses following his times in rehab, had been the only thing he could have done with the awareness he had at the time, he was able to let go of his regret and self-blame.

Instead of diminishing his sense of responsibility, it increased it. (He also let go of blaming his parents for reasons we'll come to later.) He readily acknowledged responsibility for his past actions and, more importantly, for the future. After all, he had no one left to 'blame'.

All he needed then was some new thinking to enhance his self-worth (we'll cover this in Chapter 6, 'We are who we are') and some powerful tools to take control of his life (which we'll cover in Chapter 7, 'A powerful you').

His new sense of responsibility for determining his future ensured he succeeded in grasping these tools and putting them into practice to build a new life.

What if I'm still not convinced?

Ask yourself the questions on the left below. See if you can come up with your own answers. My suggested answers are on the right.

Question	Suggested answer
Why did you do whatever you did or make the choice you made?	Because of your awareness at that moment.
What would need to have been different for you to make a different choice?	Your awareness at that moment.
How could your awareness have been different at that moment?	It couldn't have been. Something in your life history up to that moment would have had to be different.

If you're still not convinced, go back and re-read the section in this chapter headed 'Free will'.

MORE ON THE FUTURE

Even though we were doing our best, what we've done in the past doesn't need to be what we'll do in the future. Doing our best only means our best at that moment, given our awareness at the time.

A small change in attitude or ability, arising from our own thoughts or experiences, or from the advice or encouragement of others, can make all the difference to what we do in the future.

That doesn't mean we weren't doing our best before. It means our awareness has changed, so our best now is different from our best before.

But something has to happen to change our awareness. Besides receiving advice from others, from books and so on, we gain ideas from our own thoughts and experiences. So rather than saying, 'I should have done better,' we can say, 'I would have done better if I had … so I'll do better if I think this way or act this way next time.'

Won't our thoughts, feelings and actions continue to be determined by our awareness at the time? Yes they will. Does this mean we have no control over our future? Not at all.

We always have the freedom to choose, subject to any genuine constraints in our circumstances or abilities, providing we're aware that we have that choice. If we've limited ourselves in some way in the past, it's because we didn't have this awareness at the time. Even if we were aware we had a choice, we didn't have the awareness to be able to choose a different option.

But this doesn't need to be so in future.

We all have the potential to live an enjoyable, satisfying and productive life, get whatever we want out of life and contribute to others.

All we have to do is develop more productive ways of thinking or acting in the future, as we become aware that we've been limiting ourselves in the past. The more we expand our awareness, the less limited we become and the greater our freedom to choose an increasingly satisfying and productive life.

While we'll continue to do our best with the awareness we have at the time, our awareness can change dramatically in a short time. Becoming aware of this process, through reading a book such as this, is itself a change in awareness.

Life becomes like riding a surfboard. We can't always direct the wave, but as our awareness grows we can gain more control of how we ride the wave. And the more control we gain the more exciting life becomes.

CASE STUDY

Harry was disappointed with his life. He felt he'd missed out on opportunities for a better career and relationship.

Through our work together, he learned he could take control of his life, be who he wanted to be and do the things he wanted to do. But still he held back, because he feared that if he now took control, he'd regret having wasted most of his life by not taking control earlier.

Then he learned he couldn't possibly have done it earlier, given his awareness at the time. In order for that to have happened something, however small, would have had to be different in his life history.

Even to have sought my help earlier, something different would need to have happened for him to gain the awareness to do so at an earlier time.

This understanding resolved his final barrier, allowing him to totally paccept the past and start taking action to change the future.

A COMFORTABLE TRUTH?

For many this will be the first time you've come across the idea that we live in a largely determined world. Does this sit comfortably with you? Perhaps you initially thought there might be something negative about it. There's nothing negative and a huge amount that's positive in ways that will continue to unfold through this book.

It shouldn't be so surprising to hear that what we think, feel and do in any given circumstances is determined by who we are at that moment.

We're only applying this principle to the past. The past cannot be changed anyway, so this shouldn't be so challenging. Yes, what we do in the future will also be determined by our awareness at the time, but the only way we're using this aspect of the determinist idea is to understand that if we want to change what we do in the future we need to change our awareness.

And we're still saying we're absolutely responsible for our past, present and future actions, though regarding our past actions this only has implications for what we do now and in the future.

If you haven't yet fully grasped or accepted the idea, how about this for a suggestion? From what you've read so far, I hope you'll at least acknowledge that what we think, feel and do in any given circumstances is largely determined by who we are at the time.

Let's say it's 90 per cent or more determined and 10 per cent or less free will. Perhaps you'll concede it's 99 per cent or more determined and 1 per cent or less free will. Most people have spent their lives thinking and behaving as though it's the other way around. So to redress the balance, how about focusing on the determined part for a while?

The rest of this book assumes it's fully determined. So my challenge to you as you continue through the book, is to try to think and behave as though this were true. What have you got to lose? You'll have to trust me for now when I tell you that you have a great deal to gain.

DAY BY DAY

Understanding and adopting this way of thinking has an immediate impact on our lives. The examples I've given so far have focused largely on removing regret, guilt and self-blame about past events. It's also highly beneficial in dealing with day-to-day events.

When I started, I found myself using this way of thinking several times a day. It gradually became more automatic and after a while the negative thoughts just stopped arising. Practising pacceptance gradually changes our automatic ways of thinking. Here are some more examples:

- I realise I've left something at home that I need for a presentation. If a self-blaming or regretful thought enters my mind (it rarely does any more), I replace it with 'I did the only thing I could have done, so I couldn't possibly have remembered the item on this occasion.' That takes about a second. I briefly consider whether this is a 'one-off' or a pattern in my life. That may take another second. If it's a pattern I want to break, I decide what I need to do to break it, then commit to taking that action. (We'll talk more about this in Chapter 7.) If it isn't a pattern, I simply deal with the current oversight as best I can.

- I momentarily feel bad about misjudging something, perhaps while driving, causing irritation to another driver, perhaps not leaving enough time for something I need to do. I immediately acknowledge I did the only thing I could possibly have done and so let go of any momentary regret or self-blame. If it's a pattern in my life I briefly think about whether there's anything I need to change to avoid making the same mistake again.

- Any other upset, careless act or other irritation that occurs during the day that I'd once have blamed myself for, I now deal with in the same way.

- A thought enters my mind about a past mistake, such as a missed opportunity. Again, I dismiss it in the same way, using the same reasoning, and refocus on whether there's anything I need to do to make amends or avoid repeating the mistake.

I used to look back at my life and think I'd wasted various opportunities. I don't any more. I know with certainty the past couldn't have been different as I've always done my best (the only thing I could have done).

But as we'll see, the future is wide open. The future is unlimited. The future can be amazing, as indeed have been the past twenty or more years of my life since I adopted the ways of thinking and acting outlined in this book.

Exercise

Start practising right now. Whenever you have a self-blaming thought, recognise you were doing your best (or the only thing you could have done, if this works better for you).

Drop the self-blaming thought, acknowledge your responsibility and refocus on what you can do, if anything, to improve the future, if this is relevant and appropriate.

You'll have several opportunities to practise every day. If you've dropped something, forgotten something, mislaid something, or said something you'd prefer to have said differently, you were in every case doing your best (the only thing you could have done).

Apply it also to any regrets or guilt you may have about past events.

If you have a negative thought that doesn't involve self-blame, for now use the pacceptance rationale we developed in the first chapter. At the same time continue to accept any uncomfortable feelings.

So far we've only been applying the idea of doing our best to ourselves. It won't surprise you to hear that if it applies to us, it applies to others as well. In a later chapter, I'll be suggesting:

> *There's no basis for blaming others when they've annoyed, hurt or frustrated us, as they were doing their best (the only thing they could have done) with the awareness they had at the time. Indeed there's no basis for thinking in a blaming way that they should have acted differently.*

If you've been resisting what I've been telling you in this chapter, it's quite possibly because you sensed this was coming.

To allay your concerns, I'll still be saying that others are absolutely responsible for their past, present and future actions. And we can if we wish choose not to apply the principle of doing our best to acts of cruelty, undue selfishness or otherwise knowingly treating others unfairly. Nevertheless, it's going to be more challenging applying it to others than to ourselves.

To give you a chance to get used to the idea and practise on yourself, we're going to keep talking about ourselves for a chapter or two, before turning to how we view others. If in the meantime you want to go ahead and start applying it to others, be my guest.

Action summary

This chapter:

- Whenever you have a negative thought about something you've done or haven't done, understand you were **doing your best** (or the only thing you could have done) given your awareness at the time and hence given your life history up to that moment

- **Paccept** it for that reason and refocus on what you can do, if anything, to improve the future, such as not repeating it if it's a pattern you want to change

- Think about any **regrets** you may have, or guilt you may be harbouring about actions that have unintentionally hurt others, and apply the same thinking

- Acknowledge **responsibility for your past actions**, while letting go of any regret or self-blame. Understand that taking responsibility only has relevance to what you do now and in the future. Consider whether there are any actions you can take to make up for any inappropriate or ineffective actions you've taken in the past, such as apologising, making amends or committing to change your behaviour in the future

- Acknowledge your **responsibility for future actions**, including making the most of any opportunities for personal change, such as those offered by this book, for the benefit of yourself and others

Prior chapters:

- 'Accept for now' any uncomfortable **feelings** (fully experience and accept them)

- **Paccept** what is (our circumstances) at every opportunity

- Stop **worrying**

- '**Accept** the feeling, **choose** the action' to resolve recurring feelings, unproductive habits and self-limitations

- If an uncomfortable feeling keeps recurring when you've fully accepted it, **try letting it go**

- **Observe** non-pacceptance in others (TV, etc.) and consider how you'd now think and act in their circumstances

CHAPTER 6

We are who we are

"The snow goose need not bathe to make itself white. Neither need you do anything but be yourself." LAO TSE

Most of us could probably think of at least one aspect of ourselves we'd like to change if we could. We might prefer to be taller or shorter, thinner or fatter, younger, better-looking, more confident, happier, healthier, wealthier, more energetic, more knowledgeable, more capable, or more anything else.

While some of these things cannot be changed, most can, at least to some degree. But even changing these aspects of ourselves takes time. So there's little, if anything, we can change at this moment.

In this area, as in all others, accepting the things we cannot change doesn't just mean accepting the unchangeables such as our height or age. It means:

> *Paccepting ourselves totally as we are right now, at the same time as doing whatever we want to do, and are able to do, to change ourselves in the future.*

Have we any reason to think we should be different right now? We are, after all, simply the culmination of our past experiences, thoughts, choices and inherited traits – in other words our life history. And none of the things we or others have done, which have led to who we are right now, could have been different at any moment given our awareness at the time.

We can choose to change ourselves in the future if we want to and are able to, but there's no point wishing we were already different. As we and others have always been doing our best (the only thing we could have done) at every moment:

> *We couldn't possibly have been different from who we are right now.*

CASE STUDY

When Stephen realised his drug addiction and failed attempts in rehab were the only thing that could have happened given his awareness at the time, he was able to let go of regret, guilt and self-blame.

He understood that who he was right now, a drug addict dominated by self-admonishment and anger towards his parents, was the only person he could have been at that moment, given his life history – in other words, given all the decisions and choices he'd made along the way and given that those were the only decisions and choices he could have made at each moment, with the awareness he had at the time.

For the first time, Stephen was able to accept himself totally for who he was, knowing at the same time that with a small change in awareness he could change who he was and be who he wanted to be in the future.

With acceptance of himself, Stephen's sense of self-worth began to rise. With his newfound self-acceptance, his improving self-worth and his growing sense of responsibility for his past and future actions, he was willing to start using the powerful tools outlined in Chapter 7 to take charge of his life.

WE'RE ALL OK

If we could step aside for a moment and look at ourselves, the chances are we'd see someone who's always done, or tried to do, whatever seemed appropriate at the time. We'd see someone who wants to be happy but doesn't always know how, who wants to be loved but may not always feel loved, who'd like certain things out of life, but can't always seem to get them. It wouldn't be difficult to feel empathy towards such a person, whatever their shortcomings.

If we got to know this person well, heard all about their past successes and difficulties, understood their strengths and weaknesses, and shared in their hopes and fears for the future, we could doubtless grow quite fond of them.

Would he or she have to change for us to think them lovable? Probably not. We might encourage them to change in some way in the future, but that needn't be a condition for loving them now.

> *When we paccept ourselves and realise we've always been doing our best at every moment, it becomes easier to see ourselves as the lovable person we are.*

It may be worth considering why we might want to be different from the way we are right now. Could it be because we've grown up with an image of what we should be like? As long as who we are isn't unfairly hurting ourselves or anyone else, why do we need to match that perfect image?

If we're different from other people, perhaps we should treasure whatever makes us different. If we were all the same, it would be a dull old world.

Actors are generally content to play any role. They don't have to play a character with exemplary characteristics to enjoy their role. We too can choose to enjoy the character we're playing for now, with all our so-called imperfections, providing we're not unfairly hurting anyone.

If rocks could think, would they look at the stream flowing by and wish they were water? Perhaps some might. But the wise rock would probably be content being what it is. If it could find a way of changing itself into water, it might do so just for the thrill of it. But for now it would be perfectly happy being a rock.

Should a tortoise wish it was a hare so it could run faster, or the hare wish it was a bird so it could fly? I suspect tortoises and hares are content being who they are. We too can be happy being who we are right now.

Someone once said: 'The best person to be is yourself. If you try to be someone else you'll always be second best. If you're yourself, you'll be the best you there is.' We can keep changing and growing and realising more of our potential. But we can do these things from a position of being content with who we are right now.

CASE STUDY

Sarah was very overweight and had low self-esteem. Each of these problems was supported by, and contributed to, the other.

The first thing that helped her break this vicious circle was understanding that she'd always done her best (the only thing she could have done).

She then understood that, when I met her, she was the only person she could have been and her situation the only possible situation she could have been in, with the awareness she and others had at that time and at each moment in her history.

This understanding diminished her self-admonishment and her self-esteem began to improve.

The understanding that followed was that with a small change of awareness she'd be able to change her situation. The techniques we used to achieve this are described in Chapter 7.

CHANGE BECAUSE WE WANT TO, NOT BECAUSE WE NEED TO

When we see ourselves as OK just the way we are, any changes we may want to make in the future can be made out of choice and a desire to grow, rather than out of a need to be different in order to feel good about ourselves.

> *We already have everything we need to feel good about ourselves.*

We can look on any changes we may want to make in the future as a challenge. We can view them simply as part of life's adventure. It might be nice if we could snap our fingers and make those changes right now. But life isn't like that. And it would be less interesting and challenging if it were.

The challenge is to keep growing and developing, but not at the expense of paccepting who we are right now.

When we paccept ourselves as we are we can be more honest with ourselves and with others about our weaknesses, our fears and our disappointments. With those we trust, we can begin to drop any mask and try to be who we really are.

We can be more authentic, without diminishing our self-esteem and without having to protect our 'image'.

We can drop any attachment we may have to always being right. We can admit when we're wrong without feeling we're worth less as a result. And even when we think we're right, we no longer always need to prove it. We can forgo the short-term gratification to our ego of proving we're right, in exchange for the greater benefit of more satisfying relationships.

We can drop any attachment we may have to being perfect, either in the way we are, or in the things we do. We can allow for mistakes and acknowledge this as part of our natural process of growth. When we make mistakes we can smile, pick ourselves up and keep going, like a child learning to walk.

We can do things because we want to do them, rather than to win approval or admiration. We can devote more of our energy to giving love to others rather than just seeking love or approval from others. Receiving love, approval and recognition may be pleasant and even desirable, but we don't need to win approval or recognition for everything we do to feel good about ourselves.

We can be grateful for what we have, even if we might prefer to make changes in the future. If we're alive we have a great deal to be grateful for.

We can see life as an amazing gift with unlimited potential for making the most of the present and the future, whatever our circumstances might be, and for improving and expanding our future if that's what we want to do.

We're valuable human beings just being who we are. We don't need any particular attributes or successes to be valuable, though we can choose to develop those attributes and be more successful if we want to, for the benefits these things bring.

Exercise

Take a look at yourself and your life so far. See that who you are right now is simply a product of your life history. Acknowledge that you and others have always been doing your best (the only thing you could have done) and therefore who you are right now is the only person you could possibly have been at this point in your life.

Choose to paccept yourself and your life history completely. Look at the positive things you have in your life and be grateful for them. See yourself as a valuable, lovable person just the way you are, even though you may choose to make changes in the future.

CHANGING OURSELVES

If we want to change some aspect of ourselves in the future, we won't do it by wishing; we need to act.

If you want to lose weight, you won't do it by wishing you were slimmer or by feeling depressed about being overweight. You need to do something to make it happen. This needn't stop you feeling good about yourself just the way you are right now. Any action you take can be motivated by choice rather than a need to feel good about yourself.

If we feel constrained by a lack of knowledge or ability in some area, there's no point wishing we had more knowledge or ability. We can either allow our abilities to develop naturally over time, or we can take action to speed up the process. The choice is ours.

Exercise

Think of something you'd like to change about yourself. Write down the steps you need to take to achieve this. Set a date by which you'll achieve it. Select the first step you need to take and the date by which you'll take it. Then take it.

If this isn't enough to break through any constraints you may have previously experienced or that you may be feeling, wait until you've read the next chapter, called 'A powerful you'.

This is nothing surprising as far as our abilities and knowledge are concerned, but what about our unconscious programming? We've seen how our thoughts, feelings and actions are influenced by our unconscious attitudes and beliefs. Our self-confidence or self-image, the way we react and the way we relate to others, are just a few aspects of ourselves that are deeply affected by our unconscious beliefs.

These beliefs have developed as a result of our past thoughts and experiences. And they're continually being updated as a result of new thoughts and experiences. If we consistently or repeatedly think consciously in a certain way, this will eventually affect our unconscious beliefs in a similar way. So developing positive and productive attitudes will eventually have a beneficial effect on our unconscious beliefs as well.

For example, if we have a tendency to react aggressively, we may unconsciously be harbouring a fear or distrust of others. If we can develop healthy conscious attitudes, including paccepting ourselves, accepting our feelings and not blaming ourselves (or others ... which we'll address in Chapter 8) when we were only doing our best, these attitudes will in time work their way through to our unconscious and automatic ways of thinking.

There are many techniques and disciplines that can help us alter both our conscious and unconscious beliefs, and hence our ability to think and behave in more productive ways.

There are therapeutic techniques such as Cognitive-Behavioural Therapy (CBT), Acceptance-Action Therapy (AAT), hypnotherapy, Neuro-Linguistic Programming (NLP) and humanist and psychodynamic approaches.

There are positive thinking techniques, such as affirmations and visualisations. There are personal development programmes, such as Acceptance-Action Training, that use a range of techniques and philosophies to aid self-awareness and development. And there are religious disciplines and philosophies, from Western through Middle Eastern to Eastern.

This text incorporates principles from CBT, AAT and Acceptance-Action Training, which I've found in my therapy, consultancy and coaching practice to be the most effective approaches to personal change and development.

For those who are interested, the use of psychological techniques should generally be based on professional advice, while the use of other development techniques and disciplines might be based on a mixture of recommendation, personal judgement and experiment.

This text doesn't aim to include the full range of such techniques and disciplines. It's about attitudes and ways of thinking, and our resulting ways of behaving.

> *Developing positive and productive attitudes and behaviour is generally the most effective way to change ourselves.*

If there's some aspect of your life that isn't working well, the first thing to do is examine your ways of thinking and behaving. The ways of thinking and behaving we're discussing in this book have had dramatic impacts on people's lives so they might be a good place to start.

Action summary

This chapter:

- Understand that who you are right now is the **only person you could have been** since you, and others who've influenced you, have always been doing your best (the only thing you could have done), given your awareness at each moment
- **Paccept yourself** totally as you are right now
- Consider what you need to do to **develop yourself** in whatever way you wish
- Start taking **action** or wait until you've read Chapter 7, called 'A powerful you'

Prior chapters:

- 'Accept for now' any uncomfortable **feelings** (fully experience and accept them)
- **Paccept** what is (our circumstances) at every opportunity
- Recognise we were **doing our best** (the only thing we could have done) given our awareness at the time, so paccept it
- Understand we're still **responsible** for our actions, but that only impacts what we do now and in the future
- Stop **worrying**

■ 'Accept the feeling, choose the action' to resolve recurring feelings, unproductive habits and self-limitations

■ If an uncomfortable feeling keeps recurring when you've fully accepted it, try letting it go

■ Observe non-pacceptance in others (TV, etc.) and consider how you'd now think and act in their circumstances

CHAPTER 7

A powerful you

"The people who get on in this world are the people who get up and look for the circumstances they want, and if they can't find them, make them." GEORGE BERNARD SHAW

So far we've been focusing a great deal on accepting what is through a combination of accepting our feelings and paccepting our circumstances, our past actions and ourselves. We've used two rationales for pacceptance:

1 It makes no sense to wish things were already different, in other words to wish the past or present moment were different

2 They couldn't have been different anyway, since we and others have always been doing our best (the only thing we could have done) with the awareness we had at the time

We've also mentioned in a number of contexts that to change the future we need to take action:

- Pacceptance combines accepting what is with refocusing on how we can improve the future

- The pacceptance principle says if we want to change the future, we need to act

- If we find ourselves worrying we need to focus on how we can gain more control over whatever we're worrying about (while accepting 'whatever will be' to the extent we can't control it)

- To resolve recurring feelings, unproductive habits and self-limitations, we can use a powerful tool called 'accept the feeling, choose the action'

- As we've always been doing our best (the only thing we could have done) with the awareness we had at the time, if we want to change what we do in the future we need to change our awareness

- We can paccept ourselves totally as we are at the same time as taking action to develop ourselves in the future, if that's what we want to do

In this chapter we're going to look at some more powerful tools to help us take the action needed to change the future. If you're already perfectly happy with your lot in life, you may have no desire to become more powerful or to take greater control of your life. That's fine. You can skim though this chapter.

But for most, becoming more powerful and taking greater control may well be something you'd like to do. I said in the introduction, backed up by my promise, that I believe everyone can live an extraordinary life.

> *Why settle for mediocrity in any area*
> *of your life?*

Why not take control if this is something you can do, which you absolutely can? Why not be powerful? Why not determine your own future in every way that's possible? After all, we only live this life once. If you could make it amazing, which you surely can, why wouldn't you?

MAKING A COMMITMENT

If we want to change a behaviour, particularly a behaviour pattern, in our lives and the change is perceived as challenging, the way to break through that challenge is to make a commitment. If I'm helping a client to lose weight or give up smoking, drugs or any other harmful behaviour, making a commitment will be a key aspect of the solution.

A commitment is a serious and irrefutable promise to ourselves to do something, achieve something or change something.

The philosopher Goethe said:

Until one is committed there is hesitancy, the chance to
draw back, ineffectiveness. The moment one commits
oneself, providence moves too. All sorts of things occur
to help one that would never otherwise have occurred.

CASE STUDY

'Accept the feeling, choose the action' wasn't the only tool Tara needed to ensure she succeeded in reaching her target weight. To get her through the times when she felt weak and at risk of breaking her diet, she needed to make a commitment.

Tara made an irrefutable promise to herself, to me and to others close to her, that she wouldn't waiver in taking the action needed to achieve the weight she'd chosen.

When she achieved her goal, she renewed her commitment to maintain that weight to ensure she didn't backslide and regain the weight she'd lost.

Several of the examples I've given in this book from my own experience have involved making a commitment to change. Leaving earlier for important meetings and turning off my mobile when needed are small examples. Committing to do whatever was needed to achieve the things I wanted to achieve in life is a bigger one.

Exercise

Think about something, perhaps a behaviour pattern, that you want to change in your life that's challenging. Make a commitment now to do everything in your power to achieve that goal. If helpful, share your commitment with others. 'Accept the feeling, choose the action' to break through any uncomfortable feelings that may arise.

THE WHEN-THEN GAME

When we hesitate on taking action, we're often playing the 'when-then game': when my fear goes away, then I'll ...; when I no longer feel depressed then I'll ...; when I'm absolutely sure I can't fail, then I'll ... .

The trouble with the when-then game is that we keep playing it. We can always find a reason to keep hesitating. We need to:

> *Accept the feeling, choose the action,*
> *make a commitment and start*
> *taking action now.*

None of the power tools introduced in this chapter are universal. I'm not suggesting we should never say 'when... then ...'. Saying to ourselves, 'When I have the money, then I'll ...' is usually more sensible than spending money before we have it and putting ourselves in debt. But when the when-then game is getting in the way of doing something productive we need to stop playing it.

When I was thinking of starting to run seminars I found myself hesitating. 'Maybe I should leave it a while longer until I'm sure I've thought of everything.' When I realised I was playing the when-then game, I stopped hesitating and ran my first seminar.

Exercise

Are you playing the 'when-then game'? What ar_ you putting off with the excuse 'when ..., then I'll ...'? If this is true for you, and if you're honest with yourself, then you may realise it's really just an excuse for not taking immediate action, or it's a way of avoiding doing something fearful. If this is so, stop playing the game right now. 'Accept the feeling, choose the action.' If necessary, make a commitment. Start taking action now.

ACTING AS IF

Another powerful tool in our armoury is 'acting as if'. This can take a number of forms. The first way to use it is to think of someone you know and admire. Ask yourself what they would do if they were in your situation. Then 'act as if' you were that person.

CASE STUDY

Ted wanted some help with his flagging catering business. He had a good product but simply wasn't achieving the sales he needed for his business to survive.

I asked him to think of someone successful in his field who lives overseas. I then asked him to imagine this person arriving in this country, not knowing anyone but wishing to launch a successful catering business. I asked him what he thought this person would do.

Ted listed a number of things he felt sure this person would do to achieve success. It was clear that Ted wasn't doing most of the things on his list and he admitted that, by and large, this was because it would be fearful to do so.

Ted committed to 'accept the feeling, choose the action' and started working his way through the list. His business started to pick up almost immediately.

Another way of using 'acting as if' is to imagine you've already achieved your goal, whatever it may be, and ask yourself, 'How would I be behaving if this were the case?' If appropriate, start right now to act as if you've already achieved your goal.

CASE STUDY

I asked Tara how she'd be behaving differently if she'd already achieved her target weight.

She imagined the different things she'd be eating and she imagined she'd be a lot fitter and therefore more active. On my suggestion, she started acting as if this were already the case.

A third way of using 'acting as if' is to identify any negative beliefs that may be getting in the way of achieving your goal. Then think of a more positive belief that you'd like to have to replace each of the negative beliefs. Then ask yourself how you'd be behaving differently if you had this more positive belief. Start behaving that way now.

CASE STUDY

Back in the days when I was nervous speaking to groups, I had a belief that I was a nervous, and therefore ineffective, speaker.

When I started 'accepting the feeling, choosing the action' my nervousness immediately diminished. I then asked myself what I'd be doing if I believed I was a confident and capable speaker.

The answer was simply that I'd be speaking to groups a great deal more. So that was what I started doing. It won't surprise anyone who's been through this experience that this quickly had a positive impact, both on my ability as a speaker and on my self-belief.

Exercise

Review the three approaches to 'acting as if' and, if you haven't done so already, consider which is the most useful in moving you towards whatever goal you may have. Then start doing it.

TAKING BOLD ACTION

If we want to achieve a goal or change something in our lives, it may be appropriate to tackle it in small steps, one step at a time. Sometimes, however, we need to take bold action.

In the corporate world in the 1980s, continuous improvement was in vogue as a means of improving business processes. This was the approach that allowed the Japanese to continuously improve the quality of their products and so, for a while, outperform their Western rivals.

In the 1990s, re-engineering became the name of the game. Continuous improvement allows a business to improve only so far. To make even more improvement, the business may need to consider major change. This led multinational companies to consider mergers and to reorganise themselves along global lines rather than maintaining their old country-based structures.

In the corporate world this represented a major shift from one-step-at-a-time to taking bold action with resulting massive change and consequent major benefits.

Similar options apply in our own lives. We need to consider which approach seems appropriate in a particular circumstance. If one-step-at-a-time is not getting us to where we want to be, we may need to consider taking bold action.

CASE STUDY

Peter was 22 years old and had never had a girlfriend. He was shy and reserved and felt ashamed that this had led to missed opportunities.

The idea that he could 'accept the feeling, choose the action' was a breakthrough for him and gave him strength. He also recognised he'd been playing the 'when-then' game – 'when I'm more confident, then I'll …'.

I thought he now had the tools he needed to break through any limitations. But when Peter heard about taking bold action, he decided to go further. He committed to a string of activities that he felt would move him more quickly to his goal.

He signed up for speed dating, a singles dinner club and a singles holiday. He subsequently had to cancel the holiday, as before he was due to go, he was already in a relationship.

Taking bold action may be fearful. If this is so, but we still know it's the right thing to do, we need to:

> *'Accept the feeling, choose the action',*
> *make a commitment, stop playing*
> *the when-then game, act as if*
> *and take bold action.*

Exercise

Is there something you want to change or achieve that you've not achieved, and think you may not achieve by taking a 'one-step-at-a-time' approach? Is it more likely to be achieved by taking bold action?

> If the bold action you need to take is safe enough, what's stopping you? If it's fear, then 'accept the feeling, choose the action'. If it's challenging, make a commitment. If you're playing the 'when-then' game, choose to stop playing it. If you can think of someone who would take bold action in your situation then act as if you're that person.
>
> Plan the bold action you need to take. Then take it.

FOCUSING ON CONTRIBUTION

If we find ourselves stuck on achieving a goal or making a change, it often helps if we can refocus on what the goal or change will contribute to others, rather than just what we can get out of it ourselves.

> *Contribution is often a more powerful motivator than self-advancement.*

In my own example of hesitating when I was thinking of presenting seminars, I realised I was focusing on myself. Was I ready? Was I sufficiently prepared? Would I succeed? When I switched my focus to what I could contribute to others, there was no longer any reason to hesitate.

It was clear to me that I was ready enough and prepared enough to give huge benefits to others. Hesitating because of my own concerns was denying others those benefits. With this realisation I stopped hesitating and took action.

Exercise

Is there something you want to achieve in your life? Are you hesitating? Could this be because you're look- ing at the challenge just from your own perspective – your fears, your skills, your readiness?

Would it help if you focused on the contribution you could make to others rather than the benefits and challenges for yourself? Try changing your focus to the benefits others would gain. See if this makes the difference, combined with the other power tools we've discussed, to initiate action.

SETTING GOALS

If there are things we want to achieve or change in our lives, setting goals can help. Think about whether there's anything you want to change or achieve in any of these areas:

- Work, career and finance
- Health, body, fitness
- Family and friends
- Relationships
- Hobbies and interests
- Spirituality
- Personal development

Here are some useful questions to help you identify worthwhile goals:

ake you out of your comfort zone?

; do you want to break?

to write down our goals. For each goal you come up with, ask yourself the following questions and write down the answers. You can make columns on a sheet of paper with your goals in the left column and abbreviations of these questions as column headings.

- What are the benefits?
- By when will I achieve the goal?
- Am I willing to:
  - Accept the feeling, choose the action?
  - If it's challenging, make a commitment?
  - Stop playing the 'when-then game'?
  - Act is if?
  - Take bold action?
  - Focus on contribution?
- What's the first/next step I need to take?
- By when will I take it?
- Do I need any support?

Then start taking action.

If we use all the above tools, there really isn't much we can't achieve if we want to:

- Yes you really can be successful in your chosen career and be financially successful if that interests you
- Yes you absolutely can be the weight you want to be

- Yes you definitely can give up smoking if that's what you want to do

- Yes you truly can improve your relationships (see later chapters) if you put your mind to it

And yes you really can do whatever it takes to develop yourself in all the ways outlined in this book, if that's what you choose to do.

That too is a **promise**.

A TURNING POINT

This chapter has the potential to be a turning point in your life. Don't waste that opportunity. As I said at the beginning of the chapter, if you're totally comfortable with your life as it is, then clearly you don't need to change it. But if there's something you want to change or achieve, now is your chance. Do whatever it takes.

If you've already committed to taking action in one or more of the above exercises, great. If you haven't, what's stopping you? At some point you'll need to take action. So why not now?

You can keep reading this book and gain plenty more life-changing tools, but what's stopping you committing to action now? If it's fear, procrastination or lack of self-belief, accept the feeling and commit anyway.

- If you want to advance your career, take action to achieve that now. If the action you want to take is sensible but fear or reticence is standing in your way, accept the feeling, choose the action and make a commitment.

■ If you want to lose weight, accept any feelings and commit to taking action now. Or take action to get the professional help you think you might need. If later you're tempted to deviate from your diet and exercise pro-gramme, accept the feeling and choose to maintain your commitment. If you're wanting to eat when you're not hungry, accept the desire and choose not to eat.

■ If you want to give up smoking, do it now. Make a com-mitment right now never to smoke again … ever. Or take action to get the professional help you think you might need. If once you've given up you feel like a cigarette, accept the desire and choose not to indulge it.

■ If there's anything you're fearful of, take action now to break through the fear, or commit to taking that action as soon as this is feasible. Accept the fear and choose to do whatever you're afraid of.

■ If you had no fear and total self-belief, what would you be doing differently in your life from what you're doing now? Choose to start acting right now as if you already have no fear and total self-belief. Accept any fear or other feelings and choose to take bold action to make it happen.

In all these cases, consider how others will benefit from the change you're going to make. Now make it.

Action summary

This chapter:

If you have something you want to change or achieve in your work or your life, consider whether any or all of the following are applicable:

- **Commit** to taking action
- Stop playing the **when-then** game
- Act **as if**
- Take **bold action**
- Focus on **contribution**
- Set **goals**

Then start taking action.

Prior chapters:

- 'Accept for now' any uncomfortable **feelings** (fully experience and accept them)
- **Paccept** what is (our circumstances) at every opportunity
- Recognise we were **doing our best** (the only thing we could have done) given our awareness at the time, so paccept it
- Understand we're still **responsible** for our past actions, but that only impacts what we do now and in the future
- **Paccept ourselves** totally as we are, at the same time as seeking to develop
- Stop **worrying**
- '**Accept** the feeling, **choose** the action' to resolve recurring feelings, unproductive habits and self-limitations
- If an uncomfortable feeling keeps recurring when you've fully accepted it, **try letting it go**
- **Observe** non-pacceptance in others (TV, etc.) and consider how you'd now think and act in their circumstances

CHAPTER 8

Blaming them

"Loving those who agree with our views is easy. Loving those who don't is true love." ERIC FROMM

If we've always been doing our best (the only thing we could have done) at every moment, given our awareness at the time, then so have others.

> *Even when others have annoyed or frustrated us, seemed unreasonable, petty, argumentative or unfriendly, or have inconvenienced us through their carelessness or inability, they were doing their best (the only thing they could have done) at that moment, given their awareness at the time.*

We've all behaved inappropriately at times in the eyes of others, because at that moment we didn't know how to, weren't able to, or didn't think we ought to, behave differently.

We probably thought we were behaving appropriately even if others didn't think so. We may have acted aggressively or unreasonably because we were upset about something. Whatever it was, we were doing our best at that moment in the circumstances, given our awareness at the time. And so were others.

They're still responsible for their actions (we'll discuss this shortly). And if I want to, I can choose not to apply the principle of doing our best to acts of cruelty, undue selfishness or otherwise knowingly treating others unfairly. But most people don't act in cruel or knowingly unfair ways.

In fact we can always choose when to apply the principle and when not to. The behaviour of others is sometimes so appalling, we may choose not to think of them as having done their best given their awareness at the time. But again, most people don't behave in appalling ways.

If another motorist has been inconsiderate, if someone has said something that's annoyed us, if a work colleague has been uncooperative, if we think we've been unjustly criticised, if an official has done something we view as incompetent or if the buses aren't running on time, those involved were all doing their best (the only thing they could have done) at each moment.

I'm not suggesting we should stop criticising others. But if we're aware they were doing their best, it becomes a great deal easier to criticise constructively and in a less blaming way.

> *Criticising others in a blaming way is generally counter-productive, even if we do object to, or disagree with, their actions.*

We should still hold others responsible and therefore accountable for their actions. But blaming them for their failings or weaknesses implies they chose them.

As I said in Chapter 5, most of us don't consciously choose our characteristics. They develop over time, as a consequence of our thoughts and experiences and the choices we make along the way.

We each have the power to change our attitudes. But we can only make this choice if we're aware of how we're behaving, can see a reason to change, and have the will and the ability to do so.

We may sometimes need help to achieve these things, such as constructive advice and criticism from others. But being criticised for our faults or weaknesses in a blaming way usually doesn't help. If anything, it only makes us defensive and less willing to change. The same is true of others.

When we stop blaming others for their failings and weaknesses, we can view their actions more objectively, instead of judging the person subjectively.

If we've been inconvenienced or put out by someone's lack of ability, we can see it for what it is – a lack of ability in that area, without having to remain annoyed or upset if that's how we've initially reacted. The same applies if we've been put out by someone's attitudes or some aspect of their personality.

We all have a tendency to judge others by comparing their behaviour with our own. This may sometimes be a reasonable basis for judging their behaviour, but is it a reasonable basis for judging the person?

Would it be reasonable for someone exceptionally capable, socially adept and industrious to judge the rest of us in a blaming way for having fewer of these attributes? Is it any more reasonable for us to judge others in a blaming way because we think they have fewer attributes in some area than we have?

CASE STUDY

Stephen's problem with drugs was closely linked to anger towards his parents.

As a first child, Stephen had not reacted well to the arrival of his sister and, as often happens with eldest children, had vented his sense of betrayal by becoming rebellious and difficult.

His father had perhaps been overly assertive and punitive in response, which Stephen grew to resent. He was angry with his mother too, for not protecting him from his father's excesses.

Stephen's drift into drug taking was just another form of rebellion and his relapses following rehabilitation, paid for by his parents, were to some extent more of the same.

When Stephen understood that, despite any failings, his parents had always done their best in the circumstances, with the awareness they had at the time, and indeed both he and his parents had always done the only thing they could have done, given their awareness at each moment, his anger and resentment began to diminish.

Stephen was able to let go of the blame he felt towards both himself and his parents, and for the first time he began taking total responsibility for his future.

Using the 'power tools' outlined in the previous chapter, Stephen began taking charge of his life, making decisions and taking actions that quickly turned his life around.

If a playful puppy knocks over a vase, we may feel frustrated or irritated. But these reactions soon subside. We won't harbour resentment towards the puppy, because we know it wasn't intentionally acting irresponsibly. If we can appreciate that others were also doing their best given their awareness at the time, our feelings of frustration and annoyance won't develop into resentment.

BLAME AND RESENTMENT

Blame and resentment are at the core of much of the unhappiness, dissatisfaction and destructive conflict in the world. History is full of them. We read about them in newspapers and see them on television. People who lead otherwise successful lives are made miserable by them. And to the extent that we experience unnecessary blame and resentment, our own lives are also diminished.

We may blame our parents, husbands, wives or children for the things they've done when, at the time, they thought they were doing the right thing, or they didn't have the awareness, the will or the ability to do better.

We may resent our boss, or any other authority figure, for the things they've done or haven't done when they too were simply doing their best (the only thing they could have done) at the time.

If we can diminish blame and resentment in our lives we'll be happier for it and can concentrate on more productive thoughts and actions.

THEY'RE STILL RESPONSIBLE

We're not letting others off the hook. They're still responsible for their actions. Diminishing blame doesn't mean we stop holding others responsible and accountable.

They alone control their actions and they alone choose them. We're all responsible and accountable for our actions and can commit to acting more responsibly in the future if we've acted irresponsibly in the past.

As I said in Chapter 5, blame focuses on the past; responsibility focuses on the future.

Blame involves wanting the past to be different or thinking it 'should have been different', which is a nonsense both because it can't now be different (what is, is) and because it couldn't have been different anyway if everyone involved was doing their best (the only thing they could have done) at the time.

Responsibility is about what happens now and in the future. For example:

- Holding others responsible for their past actions can impact what they do now in relation to those past actions. They may be persuaded to make amends, apologise or take action to ensure it doesn't happen again.
- Holding others responsible might mean taking action to protect ourselves, such as removing them from office or putting them in prison so they don't repeat what they did and so others may be dissuaded from taking similar action.

So if you're thinking of bringing a psychologist or philosopher into court to explain to the judge that you were doing your best (the only thing you could have done) at the time, think again. It's unlikely to be an effective defence.

■ Knowing that others will hold us responsible for the actions we take now will hopefully affect how we think and behave right now. We've said what we do in a particular set of circumstances is determined by our awareness at the time. Knowing others will hold us responsible is one of the circumstances that will impact our awareness.

Hopefully my awareness of the dangers of speeding will be sufficient to persuade me not to speed. But knowing I'll be held responsible and accountable by way of a fine and endorsement is likely to be an additional influence.

If we're blaming the gas company for poor service we're likely to get irritated or upset. Understanding everyone involved was doing their best (the only thing they could have done), yet still holding them responsible, might involve writing a letter to influence their awareness or taking our business elsewhere to protect our own interests.

If others have been cruel, unduly selfish or knowingly unfair and are not willing to take responsibility, including changing their behaviour and, where appropriate, making amends, I could choose not to apply the principle that they were doing their best. But most people aren't cruel, unduly selfish or knowingly unfair to others.

AND SO TO PACCEPTANCE

Recognising others were doing their best (the only thing they could have done) is a powerful justification for paccepting their actions.

> *We can choose to paccept what others have said or done, not just because there's no point wishing things were already different, but also because they were doing their best (the only thing they could have done) at that moment.*

So when any annoyance or frustration we may initially feel has subsided, we can avoid perpetuating the thoughts that generated those reactions.

CASE STUDY

As a child, Maria had always been close to her father. After Maria's mother died from an illness, her father remarried. Maria didn't get along with her new stepmother.

Maria blamed her father for 'deserting' her. She left home and, when I saw her, hadn't spoken to her father for many years.

Each blamed the other for the rift and neither was prepared to break the ice. The truth is that each had always behaved in the only way they knew how at each moment, with their own personal histories and hence their awareness at the time.

When Maria understood this, and realised that both her father and stepmother, as well as herself, had all done the only thing they could have done with their awareness at the time, she was able to paccept what had happened and reconnect with her family.

THE PRESENT TOO

In Chapter 5, I mentioned that I don't apply the principle of doing our best to my own actions in the present moment because as soon as we try to, our awareness changes.

But we can apply it to others in the present moment. In other words it's true that others are doing their best (the only thing they could be doing) right now, given their awareness at this moment. After all, our realising this doesn't change their awareness.

The next time you're having a disagreement with someone or feel irritated about something they're saying or doing, stop and think about what they're saying or doing and understand that it's the only thing they could be saying or doing right now.

This has some big implications for how we might deal with our own reactions. We'll look at this in the next chapter.

I'M NOT SAYING

It may be helpful if I mention a few things I'm **not** saying:

- I'm not suggesting we should always avoid getting angry or upset with others. Getting angry or upset is part of being human. What I **am** suggesting is that we don't have to remain angry or upset, unless we believe this to be warranted – as we may well do, for example, when we witness or hear about extreme cruelty or injustice.

- I'm not saying we should let others get away with unreasonable behaviour. Even if they were doing their best given their awareness at the time, that doesn't mean we have to 'put up with it' and let them carry on behaving that way. We can tell them how their behaviour makes us feel, we can ask them to behave differently, or we can go somewhere where their behaviour won't affect us.

- I'm not advocating a 'softer' approach towards maintaining or encouraging proper standards of behaviour. On the contrary, societies need firm guidelines on acceptable standards, supported by action to enforce them where appropriate. As we've said, holding people responsible and accountable in a punitive way for unacceptable behaviour is one way of encouraging better attitudes and behaviour.

- And I'm not saying we should like everyone. They may have always been doing their best given their awareness at the time, but we may not like their awareness and therefore the way they think and behave.

But pacceptance encourages a more objective response to undesirable behaviour in place of blame and resentment.

UNDERLYING REASONS

Paccepting what others have said or done becomes easier if we remember there's always a reason for their behaviour, though we may not know what it is.

In fact, we usually don't know the underlying reasons. We only see the apparent reasons. If someone reacts in an unfriendly way to some apparently harmless thing I've said or done, the reason for their behaviour may appear to be whatever I said or did. But the underlying reasons lie in their attitudes, personality and abilities, and hence in their life history, which caused them to react in that way. What I said or did was simply the catalyst that triggered their reaction.

Since we're usually unaware of the underlying reasons, we tend to judge other people's behaviour on the basis of the apparent reasons. So we view them as being unreasonable.

CASE STUDY

If I'm receiving poor service in a restaurant, I may react by feeling frustrated or annoyed. But if I remain dissatisfied I'll simply spoil my own enjoyment of the meal. If I can see the waiter was doing his best (the only thing he could have done) given his awareness at the time, I can more easily avoid remaining dissatisfied.

Perhaps he dislikes his job and doesn't have the confidence, motivation or abilities to find another one. He might be new to the work and simply doesn't know how to do it well.

Maybe he has problems at home and doesn't know how to avoid bringing them to work. Perhaps he's generally unmotivated, or carries a chip on his shoulder, and hasn't the will or the ability to do something about it.

Whatever the explanation, there's no point wishing the situation were already different. If I want to do something constructive I can speak to the waiter, without needing to attack him personally. I can reinforce the message by not leaving a tip. Or I can give the manager my opinion and leave him to decide what to do.

And if I think the restaurant is poorly managed, I can choose not to eat there again.

We don't need to unravel the underlying reasons for everyone's behaviour. But being aware that there are underlying reasons can help us to view others in a less negative way.

Recognising others were doing their best doesn't mean putting up with poor performance or leaving people in jobs they aren't able to do. On the contrary, when we take a more objective view of other people's performance and abilities, it becomes easier to communicate our views to whoever is in a position to do something about it.

CRITICISM AND STANDARDS

When we criticise others it's only fair to consider whether our criticism is objective. Does the other person's behaviour fall short of standards that most reasonable people would support, or does it just fall short of our own standards or ideas? If it's the latter, we might still want to express our views but we might also want to be more cautious before we criticise.

If we find ourselves disagreeing with other people's views, we can still respect those views. Is it reasonable for us to criticise others simply because their beliefs or opinions differ from our own? Our beliefs and opinions are based on our backgrounds and our past thoughts and experiences. So it's inevitable that others will hold beliefs and opinions that differ from our own.

Debating our differing views is healthy. Criticising others simply because we disagree with them denies the inevitable differences in our backgrounds and experiences.

CASE STUDY

I belong to the half of humanity that squeezes toothpaste tubes from the bottom. I used to feel mildly irritated if someone from the other half of humanity squeezed my tube in the middle.

Would I have been justified in thinking the middle squeezers were wrong? I hardly think so. They're just as entitled to their view of toothpaste squeezing as I am to mine.

I might have tried to persuade my tormentors of the benefits of becoming bottom squeezers. But I'd hardly have been justified in thinking badly of them.

PERSPECTIVES

Nothing we say or do ever seems unreasonable from our perspective, at least at the time. And nothing others say or do seems unreasonable from their perspective, however unreasonable we think they're being. So if we want to understand or influence those we disagree with, it helps if we can try to see the issue from their perspective.

When conflicts arise, whether between individuals, nations, races, religions or other interest groups, each side naturally believes itself to be right and the other to be wrong. Each side has no shortage of arguments and justifications for its own position and gives little credence to the arguments and justifications for the other's position.

But if each can appreciate that the other's position appears reasonable to them, any destructive resentment that may otherwise fuel the conflict can be diminished. Aggression, retaliation and stubbornness are fuelled by resentment.

Understanding that our adversaries believe they're right, just as we do, may not resolve the conflict. But it can reduce the unhappiness and damage the conflict may otherwise cause and make the parties more willing to settle their differences.

CASE STUDY

Alan and Rita were thinking of separating. They'd been arguing a great deal. Alan thought Rita was controlling, Rita thought Alan was uncaring. Their differences had developed into resentment. The positive aspects of their relationship had been largely forgotten.

In therapy we set a rule that a problem could only be aired if the person airing it first described it from the other person's perspective. Each of them found this both challenging and revealing.

They were both experiencing regret and some guilt about the way their relationship had deteriorated. When they understood they'd always been doing their best (the only thing they could have done) with the awareness they had at the time, this regret and guilt was resolved.

Understanding that the other person had similarly always been doing their best (the only thing they could have done) at each moment was also a revelation. It greatly diminished their resentment and, together with practising viewing issues from their partner's perspective, led to a resolve to work things out, be more responsive to each other's needs and refocus on the positive things about their relationship.

One or both parties in a conflict may be driven by selfish motives. But even those whose motives are selfish usually develop arguments to convince themselves that they're in the right. I'm not condoning selfish behaviour. Blatantly selfish acts that unfairly disadvantage others need to be resisted and are worth getting upset about. But in trying to settle conflicts it usually helps if we can try to understand the other side's perspective or point of view.

I-STATEMENTS

When we drop any resentment we may feel towards someone we're in conflict with, it becomes easier to use 'I-statements' as an alternative to criticism. Criticism after all generally achieves little, as the person being criticised will usually become defensive.

An I-statement means letting the other person know, in a non-blaming way, how we feel. It has to be genuinely non-blaming, using words such as 'I'm not blaming you and I'm not saying you have to change, I'm just letting you know how I feel.'

Unless the relationship has reached the point where one party wants to hurt the other, an I-statement is usually more likely to achieve a positive response, since the recipient no longer feels attacked and so no longer needs to be defensive.

FORGIVENESS AND RECONCILIATION

Forgiveness is a powerful mechanism for resolving resentment and the ability to forgive is generally an admired attribute.

Pacceptance, based on the understanding that we've all been doing our best at every moment with the awareness we had at the time, can facilitate forgiveness. Pacceptance can also be an alternative, as once we paccept the person or their behaviour, there may be little left to forgive.

Either way, pacceptance and forgiveness go hand in hand. Where applicable either, or both, can lead to reconciliation.

CASE STUDY

Donna had separated from her husband some years before I met her. Yet her life was still dominated by memories and resentment of his abusive behaviour. He had been physically violent during their marriage.

She already knew that her husband had been abused as a child, but she saw this as no excuse for his behaviour. I agreed with her. While his childhood might be a reason for his behaviour, it was certainly no excuse. He was totally responsible for his actions.

Nevertheless, Donna found it helpful to understand that her husband had always done his best (the only thing he could have done) with the awareness he had at the time, however disturbed his awareness might have been.

She chose to adopt this way of thinking despite viewing his behaviour as often cruel and selfish.

With the help of this understanding, Donna was able to forgive her husband. She then chose to restore communication, primarily for the sake of her children.

If you've fallen out with someone you'd like to reconcile with, these might be some useful aspects of a reconciliation:

■ Recognise you were both doing your best (the only thing you could have done) with the awareness you had at the time

■ Let the other person know, in a non-blaming way, how you felt or feel

■ Apologise for your part in whatever happened

Hopefully the other person will reciprocate. It may help if they've read this book.

Exercise

Think about someone whose behaviour you've resented in the past and perhaps still do. See if you can identify the attitudes, unconscious programming and abilities that influenced their behaviour. Try to see the situation from their perspective.

If they weren't being cruel, unduly selfish or knowingly and intentionally unfair to others, acknowledge they were doing their best (the only thing they could have done) given their awareness at the time. Paccept it and choose to drop any resentment you may have held on to until now.

If you're still in a relationship with this person, or would like to renew contact if this had been lost, consider whether you're willing to clear up any misunderstanding. Then take action to do it. If it's fearful, accept the feeling, choose the action.

IDENTIFYING WITH GROUPS

When conflicts arise between groups it helps to keep in mind the arbitrary ways in which we come to identify with groups. We're all born into a family, community, race and nation. We may join or support organisations, religions, sports teams and so on. If our group is in conflict with another, we naturally tend to identify with our own group and see members of the other group as adversaries.

But as individuals we usually aren't so different from those in the other group. We probably have the same needs and drives and similar ideas on fairness and justice. The main difference between us is that we identify with a different group and so our perspective is biased in favour of that group. Recognising this can help to diffuse the conflict.

For some readers, this may have been the most challenging chapter so far. If others have done things that have greatly upset you and perhaps you've resented, it's not always easy to make the shifts in thinking we've outlined in this chapter.

It can take time to absorb these ideas sufficiently to enable you to let go of upset or resentment.

If this is the case for you, don't be hard on yourself. It will probably help if you practise on smaller day-to-day issues before tackling the bigger issues in your life. Some day-to-day examples are given at the end of the next chapter.

Action summary

This chapter:

In any challenging situation involving the actions of another person or organisation:

- Understand they were and are **doing their best** (the only thing they could have done or could be doing right now) given their awareness at the time, and hence given their life history up to that moment
- **Paccept** what they've done or are doing on that basis, if you prefer, as long as they weren't being cruel, unduly selfish or otherwise knowingly unfair to others

- Recognise they're still **responsible** for their actions, but that only impacts what happens now and in the future

- Try to understand their behaviour from their **perspective**

- Offer **constructive** suggestions or criticism if you believe this is warranted

- **Paccept/forgive** others for their past actions if appropriate

- **Reconcile** with significant others if needed

Prior chapters:

- 'Accept for now' any uncomfortable **feelings** (fully experience and accept them)

- **Paccept** what is (our circumstances) at every opportunity

- Recognise we were **doing our best** (the only thing we could have done) given our awareness at the time, so paccept it

- **Paccept ourselves** totally as we are, at the same time as seeking to develop

- '**Accept** the feeling, **choose** the action' to resolve recurring feelings, unproductive habits and self-limitations

- **Commit**; stop playing the **when-then** game; act **as if**; take **bold action**; focus on **contribution**; set **goals** where needed to make changes, address goals and challenge ourselves

- Stop **worrying**

- If an uncomfortable feeling keeps recurring when you've fully accepted it, **try letting it go**

- **Observe** non-pacceptance in others (TV, etc.) and consider how you'd now think and act in their circumstances

CHAPTER 9

It's all about me

"Most people are about as happy as they make up their minds to be." ABRAHAM LINCOLN

OWNING OUR REACTIONS

If I had a fear of mice would that mean mice were dangerous? Not at all. Mice, after all, are just mice. My fear would have more to do with the way I've learned to think about mice, together with my unconscious programming. The sight of a mouse would simply be the trigger for my programmed reaction to mice.

When I see a mouse I might think there's something dangerous or inherently frightening about mice. We tend to project our reactions onto the situations, things or people that trigger them and view them as the cause of our reaction.

> *But if we can take 'ownership' of our reaction, that is acknowledge that it's primarily a function of our own unconscious programming and automatic ways of thinking, we can see the situation more objectively.*

We can see it for what it really is: a harmless mouse that triggers a reaction in me because of the way I've become programmed to react to mice.

Not all situations we react to are as harmless as mice. But most come pretty close.

There's nothing inherently frustrating about a traffic jam. A traffic jam is just too many cars trying to fit into too small a space. If I feel frustrated when I'm stuck in one, this has more to do with my expectations about how the traffic should be moving and the workings of my unconscious programming and automatic ways of thinking when these expectations aren't met.

There's nothing inherently annoying about someone disagreeing with me. It's simply someone expressing views that are different to my own. If I feel irritated, it's probably because of how, consciously or unconsciously, I'd prefer my views to be received by others.

PAST PROGRAMMING

Our reactions may not always result from a particular expectation. Our unconscious mind sometimes replays records of past painful experiences, mainly from childhood. These records can be triggered by events that unconsciously remind us of those experiences.

If we had a painful experience when we felt unjustly criticised as a child, we may be particularly sensitive to criticism as an adult. If we had an unpleasant experience when we were the centre of attention as a child, we may experience a nervous reaction when we're the centre of attention as an adult.

But whatever the cause, our reactions are primarily a function of our own unconscious programming and automatic ways of thinking.

> *The situation we're reacting to is simply the trigger for our reaction.*

As we said in Chapter 1, this doesn't mean we should or could have avoided reacting, at least as far as our automatic thoughts and feelings are concerned. We can't immediately avoid our automatic ways of thinking or resulting feelings.

But owning our reactions, in other words seeing them as primarily a function of our own programming, can allow us to see the situation more objectively.

THE BENEFITS

Owning our reactions isn't always useful. If I come face to face with a hungry-looking tiger, I'm likely to experience a strong desire to flee. My reaction is still a function of my unconscious programming and automatic ways of thinking. But being aware of this is fairly academic when choosing between fleeing or being eaten.

My reaction to hungry tigers is a productive one. A similar reaction to mice might not be so productive. Our lives are full of reactions, some of which are productive and some of which aren't. It would be a cold world if we didn't feel sadness over the suffering of others, grief when we lose a loved one, or anger when we witness cruelty or injustice. Owning these reactions may offer little benefit. But owning our less productive reactions can be hugely beneficial.

When we own our reactions, we can see our reactions and whatever we've reacted to separately, and view them independently, even though one may have triggered the other. If we can view whatever we've reacted to independently of our reaction, we can see it for what it really is, rather than just seeing it through our reaction.

If I view an elephant through blue-tinted glasses, the elephant may appear blue. But if I'm aware of what's really going on, I can think about the elephant and the glasses separately. I can see them as they really are, a grey elephant and blue-tinted glasses.

If a careless driver has annoyed me and I just view him through my annoyance, I'll see him in a pretty negative light. But if I can own my reaction (recognise it's primarily a function of my own unconscious programming and automatic ways of thinking) I can view the driver and my reaction separately. I can see them for what they really are, a careless but probably well-meaning driver, and my own programmed reaction.

> *If I can make myself aware that my reaction is my own issue, and accept any uncomfortable feelings, then my reaction will usually immediately subside. Once it's subsided, I can more easily paccept the person or situation I've reacted to.*

CASE STUDY

Mark loved his wife but was irritated by certain things she did, often resulting in him saying hurtful things in response, which in turn led to pointless arguments. He blamed her behaviour for the problem.

When he learned to start taking ownership of his reactions, he was able to focus on, and accept, his feelings, rather than being compelled to respond.

He was then able to share how he was feeling with his wife in a more constructive way and in return she began moderating the behaviours that upset him.

A word of caution. Owning our reactions doesn't mean we have no responsibility for the reactions we trigger in others. So suggesting others own their reactions when we've upset them would be neither justified nor productive.

CHOOSING OUR RESPONSE

Owning our reactions and accepting our feelings help us to paccept the situation and so enables us to choose a more productive response.

A 'response' is those thoughts that are under our control, together with our actions, which are always under our control, whereas a 'reaction' is our automatic thoughts and feelings. Our reactions are automatic, whereas we can always choose our response.

CASE STUDY

If I'm waiting at a slow-moving supermarket checkout and I'm running short of time, I may be feeling frustrated or annoyed with the checkout staff, or with the other customers for being slow. Or I may be feeling annoyed with myself for choosing a bad time to be in the supermarket.

As long as I view the situation as the prime cause of my reaction, I may remain frustrated or annoyed. But if I can own my reaction, and view the situation I'm reacting to separately, I can see each more objectively.

I may well decide the staff or other customers are being slow, or that I chose a bad time to be there. If there's something I can do to change these things (such as changing my mind and leaving), I may do it.

Understanding that the staff and customers are doing their best given their awareness at the time, and that I was doing my best when I chose to be there at this time, will help.

Paccepting the situation will in turn avoid perpetuating the thoughts that generated my annoyance or frustration in the first place.

Owning our reactions, accepting our feelings and paccepting the situation help us to choose a more productive response. For example, I can avoid saying anything unproductive as a result of my reaction.

Exercise

Recall something that's annoyed, frustrated or upset you in the past. See your reaction as primarily a function of your own automatic thoughts and unconscious programming.

If it was another person you were reacting to, acknowledge that both of you were doing your best (the only thing you could have done) given your awareness at the time. Choose to paccept the situation as something that cannot be 'unhappened' and couldn't have been different.

Consider what your response might have been, or could be in the future, with this awareness.

TAKING CONTROL

We've now explored a number of tools. Owning our reactions, accepting our feelings, paccepting what is and paccepting ourselves and others enable us to choose the way we experience our circumstances at any moment. (Owning our reactions is now first in the list because this is often the first thing we need to do.)

Choosing our actions (accept the feeling, choose the action; make a commitment; stop playing the when-then game; act as if; take bold action; focus on contribution) and choosing a productive response enable us to take greater control of our circumstances.

We can't always control our circumstances, though we can go a long way towards it. But we can always choose, and so take control of, how we 'experience' our circumstances, whatever they may be.

We can begin by taking responsibility for the way we experience any situation in our lives. We can do this by recognising that our unhappiness or dissatisfaction in any situation is a result of the way we're thinking. The situation after all is what it is and couldn't have been different if everyone involved was doing their best (the only thing they could have done).

Taking responsibility for our experience means making statements, or wording our thoughts, in a way that recognises that it's our reaction, not the situation, that counts: 'I'm frustrated about the train being late' or 'I'm upset about the food being cold'. These statements place the responsibility for our reaction with us rather than with the event that's triggered the reaction.

Having acknowledged our responsibility for the way we experience any situation, we can start taking control of that experience by using pacceptance (accepting our feelings, paccepting what is and paccepting ourselves and others).

> *With practice we can choose the way we experience any challenging moment.*

CASE STUDY

Paul, who was trained in the use of pacceptance, was recently involved in a motor accident. He was badly injured. As he waited for the ambulance to arrive he found himself thinking about the disruption to his life and his business that the inevitable time in hospital and recovering would bring.

He knew he had a choice. He could think negatively about it or he could paccept it. It was up to him. He chose the latter. As a result he was completely unphased by the experience.

He immediately recognised both he and the other driver had done the only thing they could have done with the awareness they had at the time. (The accident was the other driver's fault but his own reflexes had been slower than they needed to be to avoid the collision.)

He accepted the pain he was in and paccepted the whole situation as just another experience in his life's journey, while he considered what needed to be done to improve his situation and maintain his business.

He sustained total pacceptance of the event and its consequences throughout his recovery.

Having taken control of the way we experience a situation, we can then take control of the situation itself, to the extent this is possible, which is something we've probably been trying to do all our lives. Where appropriate, we can use the power tools we covered in Chapter 7.

TAKING RESPONSIBILITY FOR OUR INTERACTIONS

It's fair to say that most interactions are a joint responsibility between the parties involved. It takes two to make a conflict. But viewing our interactions as a joint responsibility isn't necessarily the most productive way to view them.

In the last chapter we said that not only have others always done their best (the only thing they could have done) with the awareness they had at the time, but they're also doing so right now.

If we can understand this when we're interacting with others, especially when we're in conflict, we can appreciate that, other than a sudden realisation in the other person ...

We're the only one who can influence the other person's awareness right now. It's up to us.

Owning our reaction and accepting our feelings will diminish any reaction we may be experiencing. Understanding the other person is doing the only thing they could be doing with the awareness they have right now will diminish any negative thoughts we may have towards them.

Now we can focus on whether there's anything constructive we can do to influence their awareness, if that's what we want to do.

So it helps if we take total responsibility for our interactions. The irony is that when we're in conflict, we tend to view the interaction in quite the opposite way. We tend to hold the other person responsible in a blaming way for not seeing things the way we see them.

The truth is the other person is seeing things the only way they could be seeing them, with the awareness they have right now. The only person who has any chance of changing the way they see things is us. And we're more likely to achieve this and avoid unnecessary conflict if we take total responsibility for the interaction.

Another way of seeing this is in relation to perspective. As we said in the last chapter, we all tend to view things from our perspective. The other person of course is doing the same. And from our perspective it always seems we're right and the other person is wrong. It helps to stop and try to view any disagreement from the other person's perspective.

CASE STUDY

Stephen had come a long way. He'd changed the way he thought about his own, and his parents', past failings and so he'd been able to let go of regret and blame. He'd then applied the power tools (Chapter 7) and stopped taking drugs.

While he'd changed his own attitudes and behaviour, there were some things that hadn't changed. First, while he'd paccepted his parents' past actions, and stopped blaming them, they were still the same people and, in particular, his father was still assertive and controlling by nature.

Second, while Stephen's own programmed reactions were starting to change, he still found himself reacting to his father with frustration and occasional upset.

Stephen started practising owning his reactions. He knew his unconscious programming and automatic ways of thinking were deep-seated, based on a traumatic (for him) experience in early childhood and his whole life experience since then.

Each time he owned his reaction and accepted his feelings, he found they diminished. It was then easier for him to see his father as simply doing his best at every moment with the awareness he had at the time.

Stephen's anger towards his mother had been based on his frustration that she'd never intervened in his conflicts with his father. He now knew that she too had always been doing her best (the only thing she could have done) at each moment, with the awareness she had at the time. He also knew that her behaviour was unlikely to change.

So the only person who could influence his father's behaviour was him. He also knew his resistant/conflictual approach had never worked.

Stephen decided to try something new. For the first time in his life, he sat down with his father and talked to him in a non-blaming way. He used 'I-statements', telling his father how he felt, and had always felt, without blaming his father for those feelings. He apologised for his own rebellious behaviour and explained where he believed it had originated.

He told his father that he knew he (his father) had always done what he believed to be right. He was surprised that his father acknowledged that the same must be true of Stephen.

His father then said how impressed and thankful he was with Stephen's achievement in finally giving up drugs.

He also acknowledged that his own assertive behaviour hadn't helped. He promised to try to change.

Their relationship changed from that moment. Taking control of this aspect of his life, as of others, was another nail in the coffin of Stephen's previous low self-esteem. His life began to take off in new directions.

DAY BY DAY

Understanding and practising these ways of thinking can have a hugely positive impact on our day-to-day lives. Here are some more examples:

- Someone cuts in front of me while driving. I recognise that any irritation I feel (which is now rare) is about my own unconscious programming and automatic ways of thinking. I focus on and accept my feeling, which immediately disappears, and acknowledge to myself that the other driver is behaving in the only way he knows how with the awareness he has at this moment. I paccept it and let it go.

- I'm on my way to give a presentation overseas and have just been bumped off a flight because the airline over-booked it. I own and accept any irritation I feel, which immediately disappears. I recognise that everyone in the airline, from the policy makers down to whoever over-booked this flight and the representative who's given me the bad news, have all done their best (the only thing they could have done) at the time.

I ask the representative to convey my dissatisfaction to her superiors, in the probably vain hope that she might actually do so and the even vainer hope that this might impact on the airline's policy. Otherwise I focus only on what can be done to get me to my destination.

I later write a letter to the airline expressing my dissatisfaction with their policy and requesting recompense for the disruption. I receive a free flight as compensation but I've no idea whether I've had any other impact. Quite probably my complaint and recompense is an occasional event the airline had already taken into account in setting their policy.

REFRAMING AND GRATITUDE

There may sometimes be positive aspects of challenging situations, such as learning opportunities or, in the previous example, the possibility of a free ticket if I'm bumped off a flight. But I don't need to look for positives in order to paccept a situation.

Some people do this and find it helpful. It's called reframing, which means looking for a silver lining in any cloud to make the cloud more acceptable.

For me, silver linings are a bonus but not a necessity. While I mention it in my training, I don't teach reframing as a primary tool. The reason is that I see reliance on reframing as reinforcing the view that we can only accept something if it's positive.

For me, pacceptance is much more powerful because it can be used universally and applied immediately to any situation. I've noticed that those who rely on reframing often find it difficult to immediately identify a silver lining. But using reframing to supplement pacceptance whenever a silver lining is evident can be a helpful bonus.

In the world of personal development training, reframing has now largely been replaced by gratitude. This is taught in two very different ways. For some it's simply a new term for reframing. If we can find something positive in a negative situation, then we can be grateful for it. Once again, I treat this as a bonus rather than a primary tool.

The other way gratitude is taught is to encourage us to think about positive things in our lives and be grateful for them. For example, you could stop reading right now and write down fifty things you're grateful for in your life. Or you can end each day by thinking about something positive that's happened during the day and be grateful for it.

I find these exercises helpful and encourage you to try them, but not in place of developing pacceptance.

Exercise

If you haven't already done so, start practising owning your reactions. Every time you react to another person's behaviour, recognise your reaction is about your own unconscious programming and automatic ways of thinking and that the other person's behaviour is just the trigger.

Acknowledge the other person was or is doing their best (the only thing they could do) given their awareness at the time. Consider what you can do to influence their awareness if that's what you want to do. Or just let it go.

Recognise that how we experience events and the behaviour of others, as well as any action we take in response, is our responsibility and our choice.

Action summary

This chapter:

In every challenging situation:

- Own your **reaction** (and accept any feelings) to enable you to view your reaction and the trigger separately and paccept both
- **Take responsibility** for your experience ('I'm upset that …')
- **Choose** a more positive experience using pacceptance
- **Take total responsibility** for any interactions (the other person is doing the only thing they could be doing with the awareness they have right now)
- Choose a **productive response** (if appropriate using the power tools in Chapter 7)

Prior chapters:

- Accept for now any uncomfortable **feelings** (fully experience and accept them)

- **Paccept** what is (our circumstances) at every opportunity

- Recognise we and others were **doing our best** (the only thing we could have done) given our awareness at the time, so paccept it

- Understand we/they are still **responsible** for our actions, but that only impacts what happens now and in the future

- **Paccept ourselves** totally as we are, at the same time as seeking to develop

- Try to understand the other person's **perspective**

- **Paccept/forgive** others

- **Reconcile** with significant others

- 'Accept the feeling, **choose** the action' to resolve recurring feelings, unproductive habits and self-limitations

- **Commit**; stop playing the **when-then** game; act **as if**; take **bold action**; focus on **contribution**; set **goals** where needed to make changes, address goals and challenge ourselves

- Stop **worrying**

- If an uncomfortable feeling keeps recurring when you've fully accepted it, **try letting it go**

- **Observe** non-pacceptance in others (TV, etc.) and consider how you'd now think and act in their circumstances

CHAPTER 10

Our crazy thoughts

"There's nothing either good or bad but thinking makes it so." WILLIAM SHAKESPEARE (**HAMLET**)

Our thoughts, by which I mean our conscious thoughts, are the key to the way we experience life. Our thoughts, with the help of our unconscious programming, generate most of our feelings and actions. Our thoughts are the main determinant of our happiness or unhappiness. By and large we're happy if we're thinking happy thoughts and unhappy if we're thinking unhappy thoughts.

This book is largely about thoughts. Everything we've talked about concerns the way we think. Paccepting what is, accepting our feelings, paccepting ourselves, understanding we and others were doing our best, choosing powerful actions, owning our reactions and choosing productive responses are all ways of thinking.

We don't generally choose our thoughts and nor would we want to. Most of the time our thoughts arise spontaneously, or as a result of our circumstances and the ways we've learned to think, and there's usually no need to consciously intervene in this process.

But when we're facing difficult or challenging situations, it may pay us to look at the way we're thinking. There's nothing exceptional about this. We've all observed or been aware of our thoughts at times, just as we can observe or be aware of our feelings.

If we see that the way we're thinking isn't working in our own or other people's best interests, and we're aware of an alternative, we can choose to change our thinking in the ways we've discussed.

CHALLENGING OUR THOUGHTS

This book is mainly about challenging unproductive thinking. The basic pacceptance technique we introduced in the first chapter challenged our irrational habit of wishing things were already different. Later we applied this to worrying thoughts and to our uncomfortable feelings.

We've challenged our tendency to think we or others should have acted differently when in fact we were doing our best (the only thing we could have done) at the time. We also applied this to the way we think about who we are right now.

We've challenged our limiting beliefs using the power tools and we've challenged our urge to blame our reactions on whatever or whoever triggered them, by suggesting we own our reactions and take responsibility for them.

The full adage to live our lives by is: accept the feeling, choose the action, challenge the thought.

Here's one more technique for challenging negative thoughts that's used extensively in a therapy called Cognitive-Behavioural Therapy (CBT for short).

THOUGHT RECORDS

This tool can be used alongside pacceptance, if pacceptance alone isn't enough. It's a structured way of:

> *Challenging negative thoughts.*

If you can identify the thought behind any uncomfortable feeling, and that thought isn't resolved through pacceptance, try following the steps below. Initially it's best to write them down. With a bit of practice you can do the whole exercise quickly in your head.

- Make five columns on a piece of paper. Head the columns: 1. Thought; 2. Evidence; 3. Alternative rational thought (ART); 4. Evidence; 5. Percentage belief in the ART.
- Write the negative thought in the first column, e.g. 'I'm never going to find a job'.
- In the second column write down any evidence you can think of to support the negative thought, e.g. 'I haven't found a job yet'; 'it's hard to find a job at my age'; 'there are lots of unemployed people'.

■ In the third column, write down an equivalent positive thought. We call this an alternative rational thought (ART). You don't have to believe it right now. The thought should be whatever you think a rational positive person might think in this situation. Usually it's simply the opposite of the negative thought, e.g. 'I will find a job'. Make sure it's realistic, e.g. (at the risk of sounding ageist) if you're 80 years old, perhaps it could be 'I will find a job, even if it has to be voluntary'.

■ In the fourth column, write any evidence you can think of to support the alternative rational thought, e.g. I haven't been looking for long; others struggle to find a job and eventually succeed; it's a numbers game so I just need to apply for lots of jobs; I could try changing my strategy such as writing directly to employers; if I consult a careers counsellor I might get more ideas or find a different direction.

■ In the final column write down your percentage belief (0 to 100) in the ART. This should be your belief now while you're doing this exercise, not how you felt before.

■ Review the thought record at least once a day, add to the 'evidence for the ART' and revise the percentage belief if it changes.

■ Create more thought records for other negative thoughts.

Your belief in the alternative rational thought may initially be quite low. However, as you review the thought record repeatedly and think it through each time, your belief is likely to rise. Record your new percentage belief each time it rises.

DEALING WITH STRESS

You'll sometimes hear people suggest that a certain amount of stress is useful as it fires us up and motivates us. That really depends on our definition of stress. Stress management psychologists like myself generally define stress as a sense, belief or fear that we cannot cope. By that definition, stress is never useful and is always debilitating.

Thoughts that we cannot cope most commonly lead to feelings of anxiety, but can sometimes lead to feeling low or angry. Stress is generally debilitating while we're experiencing it, but can easily be resolved if we:

■ Accept our feelings

■ Paccept our circumstances

■ Choose whatever actions need to be taken to deal with the sources of stress

In a work context, stress can result in ineffectiveness and even absence from work. Whenever this happens the most immediate cause is usually resisting feelings that have been triggered by stressful thoughts.

The anxiety symptoms that often result from stressful thoughts can initially seem frightening. We may think there's something wrong with us. We may fear that the anxiety might grow. Generally this adds to our anxiety, which in turn compounds our stressful thoughts.

The truth is that feelings are never dangerous. They're just feelings. If we can understand this, we can accept any feelings and then paccept the circumstances that have triggered them (or, if pacceptance alone isn't enough, use a thought record) and refocus on whatever needs to be done to deal with the circumstances as best we can.

CASE STUDY

When Wendy came to see me she was suffering from insomnia (difficulty sleeping).

She'd recently taken on new responsibilities at work which were proving stressful. Her boss was putting her under pressure to deliver and she didn't believe she could meet that challenge.

She'd never heard about accepting feelings, and once she learned and applied this approach, her anxiety immediately diminished. We then addressed the thoughts that had triggered her anxiety.

She quickly learned to paccept the various aspects of her situation. She paccepted herself, her boss and her circumstances. She recognised that both she and her boss had been doing their best (the only thing they could have done) with the awareness they had at the time.

Her insomnia was driven by worry about the future and she was able to deal with this (using the various tools covered in Chapter 2), including applying pacceptance to the future, acknowledging exaggerations and focusing on the solution not the problem.

> She completed a thought record to develop a more balanced perspective of the problem.
>
> We then focused on what needed to be done to deal with the situation. She decided to be more open with her boss about her concerns and feelings. It turned out her boss was far more empathic and helpful than she'd expected.
>
> She was given the assistance and training needed to get her through the learning period until she was better able to cope with her new responsibilities.

The ideas, tools and techniques outlined in this book all build stress resilience. When you've practised them consistently for a while, you can reasonably expect to never be stressed again. If you'd like me to, I'm happy to make that another **promise**.

ACCEPTING OUR THOUGHTS

In Chapter 2 I suggested you many need to be tough with yourself by refusing to maintain a worrying thought. Similarly, it's helpful if you refuse to maintain a thought that involves 'resisting what is' by applying pacceptance. But in the early days of practising pacceptance, there may be some occasions or some area of our lives where it's difficult to change our thoughts right away, even if we want to. Our thoughts may for the moment seem dominated by our feelings. Or our unconscious programming, or conditioned ways of thinking, may be too strong for us to be able to change the way we're thinking right now.

If this is so, we shouldn't make ourselves wrong or blame ourselves, even when we recognise our current ways of thinking are unproductive. We are who we are right now. Our current ways of thinking are a product of our life history. With increased awareness, we can begin to change them, but there's no point wishing they were already different.

It's OK to have unhappy thoughts for now. There's no rule of life that says we must be happy all the time. We'd probably prefer to be most of the time, and the ideas discussed in this book will help us achieve that. But when we're unhappy or dissatisfied and we can't, or don't want to, change the way we're thinking for the time being, we can paccept that too.

If we're worried about something then, if we can accept that whatever happens will be OK, or if we can see that it probably won't happen anyway, we can stop worrying. But if we can't do this right now, we can observe ourselves worrying and know that it's OK to worry for now.

> *The truth is it's all OK. It's OK for whatever we're unhappy about to be the way it is right now. If we can paccept this, we can stop being unhappy about it. But if we can't paccept it for now, that's OK too.*

> **Exercise**
>
> Next time you're dissatisfied about something, try to make yourself aware that you're thinking unhappy thoughts, without attempting to change them. Acknowledge that it's OK to have those thoughts for now, whether or not you want to, and are able to, change them.

When we're experiencing unhappy thoughts that we can't seem to resolve right away through pacceptance or using a thought record, it's worth remembering something else about our thoughts:

> *Thoughts are just thoughts, they're not reality.*

A fear of mice doesn't mean mice are frightening. Worrying about something that may happen doesn't mean it will happen. Viewing something as a failure doesn't mean it is a failure, it just means that's the way we're viewing it.

PROFESSIONAL HELP

This book presents the most valuable ways of thinking and acting I know of that I can share with you in this way. There are other tools I use as a therapist for helping my clients deal with specific problems, which it wouldn't be appropriate to outline here.

> *If there are problems you want to deal with that aren't resolved by what you read in this book, I suggest you seek professional advice to help you work through them.*

THE STORY SO FAR

You now have a number of tools that will allow you to live your life according to the principles of acceptance-action living. If we consistently:

- Own our reactions
- Accept our feelings
- Paccept what is
- Recognise we and others were doing our best (the only thing we could have done)
- Paccept ourselves
- Choose a productive response
- Take total responsibility for our interactions
- Use the principle of pacceptance to stop worrying about the future
- 'Accept the feeling, choose the action' to resolve recurring feelings, unproductive habits and self-limitations

- Use the other power tools (see Chapter 7) to change or achieve whatever we want to change or achieve

- Use thought records where necessary to challenge our thoughts where pacceptance alone isn't enough

Then we can take complete control of our lives and our experience of life.

I meet hundreds of people through my work as a therapist, coach, consultant and trainer and in my day-to-day interactions beyond my work, who clearly don't have control over some aspect of their lives, whether it's emotional or behavioural problems, weight issues, relationships, becoming more confident, achieving more or anything else that's important to them.

They have of course always been doing their best (the only thing they could have done) with the awareness they had at the time. With the awareness you now have, you can start taking control of every aspect of your life and your experience of life. Why wait?

Action summary

This chapter:

- If pacceptance is not enough, challenge negative thoughts using a **thought record**

- Live by the adage: '**accept the feeling, choose the action, challenge the thought**'

■ If challenging a thought isn't feasible for now, **paccept the thought**:

- Acknowledge it's OK to have unhappy thoughts for now

- Recognise thoughts are just thoughts, not reality

Prior chapters:

■ Own our **reactions**

■ Accept for now any uncomfortable **feelings** (fully experience and accept them)

■ **Paccept** what is (our circumstances) at every opportunity

■ Recognise we and others were **doing our best** (the only thing we could have done) given our awareness at the time, so paccept it

■ Understand we/they are still **responsible** for our actions, but that only impacts what happens now and in the future

■ **Paccept ourselves** totally as we are, at the same time as seeking to develop

■ Try to understand the other person's **perspective**

■ **Take responsibility** for the way we **experience** every moment and **choose** our experience using pacceptance

■ Take total responsibility for our **interactions**

■ **Paccept/forgive** others

■ **Reconcile** with significant others

■ 'Accept the feeling, **choose** the action' to resolve recurring feelings, unproductive habits and self-limitations

- **Commit**; stop playing the **when-then** game; **act as if**; take **bold action**; focus on **contribution**; set **goals** where needed to make changes, address goals and challenge ourselves

- Stop **worrying**

- If an uncomfortable feeling keeps recurring when you've fully accepted it, **try letting it go**

- **Observe** non-pacceptance in others (TV, etc.) and consider how you'd now think and act in their circumstances

Note that 'owning our reactions' is now at the top of the list as it's often the first thing we need to do.

CHAPTER 11

Less wishing, more action

*"Whatever you can do or dream you can, begin it.
Boldness has genius and magic in it. Begin it now."*
GOETHE

Is there really any aspect of the world, other people, or our own lives that's at all surprising? Given the way our world and we humans have evolved, given all the events that have occurred, given the thoughts and experiences of those before us and the decisions they made, wisely or not so wisely, and given our own thoughts and experiences and the decisions we've made:

> *Why would we expect a single aspect of the world, other people or our own lives to be different from the way they were or the way they are right now?*

Yes, it would be wonderful if there were no earthquakes or floods. But, like it or not, that's the way the world is. Maybe the world would be a better place, and our lives would be easier, if others had been less unreasonable. But people are sometimes unreasonable. And yes, if I'd been born a different person, or I'd had different thoughts or experiences, my circumstances might be different. But I didn't and so they're not.

Maybe if we'd acted sooner, we could have averted a particular catastrophe. If people had acted more wisely or with greater foresight, things wouldn't have developed the way they did. If I'd thought or acted differently, I wouldn't be in my present situation. But we didn't have the awareness, the ability or the will to choose to act differently and so we didn't.

If we were able to view the past in enough detail, we could see exactly how every aspect of the world, other people and our own lives came to be the way they were or the way they are at this moment – and none of it would be at all surprising. Just as our planet has evolved the way it has through its history, so we've evolved the way we have through our history.

I don't mean it was inevitable, or that things were fated to evolve the way they did. But the choices we and others have made were hardly surprising, given our circumstances and awareness at the time, and all those unsurprising choices have combined to create the world, other people and our own lives exactly as they are at this moment.

Every situation, every action, every experience, every moment, would be unsurprising if we could view it with an understanding of everything that led up to it. It all fits together like an intricate web.

The world is the way it is because of its past. We are the way we are because of our past. If the past had been different, the present would be different. But it wasn't, so it isn't and it couldn't possibly have been.

> *We can choose to paccept the past and the present moment not only because we cannot change them and not only because we and others were doing our best (the only thing we could have done), but also because we know that if we were able to see in enough detail the complex history and inter-relationships involved, it would all be completely understandable and unsurprising.*

If someone were to suggest that mountains shouldn't be tall or that grass shouldn't be green or seagulls shouldn't fly so fast, we might think them a little strange.

Is it so different to suggest in a blaming or regretful way that we or others shouldn't have done the things we've done or that a situation should be different from the way it is right now? What is, is and there's no point wishing that what is, isn't, both because we cannot undo it and because it couldn't possibly have been different.

To say or think in a blaming or regretful way that we or others shouldn't have done what we did, or that a situation shouldn't be the way it is right now, makes about as much sense as saying it shouldn't be raining. It's raining because of the meteorological history of our planet that's led up to this moment.

> *Every situation is the way it is right now, and couldn't possibly have been different, because all the people who contributed to it were doing the only thing they could have done at every moment given their awareness at the time.*

Stop right now and read that last sentence again. Try to imagine what life might be like if you were able to think this way all the time, in every challenging situation that ever arises. Understanding that every situation you encounter in your life is the only way it could possibly have been at that moment means living with total pacceptance all the time.

CASE STUDY

Soon after I started running seminars, I arrived at a hotel one evening where the seminar was booked. I was later than usual and, as luck would have it, that was also the day when the hotel had lost the booking and nothing was prepared.

While the situation could be described as stressful, I didn't see it that way. I immediately knew this was the only situation that could have existed at that moment.

Every aspect of the situation, from me being later than usual to the hotel losing the booking, could not have been different given the awareness of everyone involved at the time. In order for it to have been different, somebody somewhere would have needed a different awareness and that wasn't possible.

Once the problem had been sorted I took action which I hoped would ensure it wouldn't happen again.

When I used this as an illustration to my audience, one participant, an experienced seminar presenter, questioned whether it was the only thing that could have happened. Surely I could have called the hotel earlier that day to ensure everything was being arranged?

It was a great suggestion but I explained that I couldn't possibly have done that for reasons which I hope by now you'll understand. But that participant had now added to my life history with his suggestion and changed my awareness, so I certainly did start calling the hotel from that day on.

WHY TWO JUSTIFICATIONS FOR PACCEPTANCE?

Knowing something couldn't have been different is generally the most powerful justification for pacceptance. But it doesn't always avoid disappointment.

Imagine you arrive home to find a meteorite has demolished your house. You might know it was the only thing that could have happened (the meteorite has probably been pointing at the piece of ground your house was built on for the last million years or so), but knowing this may still leave you disappointed.

As well as understanding it's the only thing that could have happened you may at times need to go back to the pacceptance justification we introduced in Chapter 1. Recognise you're wishing something were already different; acknowledge this is irrational because it's wishing for the impossible; drop the thought and refocus on what you can do, if anything, to improve the future.

THE CRAZIEST THING OF ALL

Imagine an alien had hitched a ride on that meteorite and, having landed on Earth, is now observing how we humans behave. Let's assume he's from a planet where everyone knows they live in a determined world and so they 'accept what is' all the time because they know that 'what is' couldn't have been different at any moment.

Our friendly alien would no doubt watch us being upset by situations and getting upset with each other, being dissatisfied with our circumstances, getting stressed by events, worrying about the future and getting into conflict. He'd probably be intrigued by all this bizarre behaviour.

Maybe he'd be thankful to have spent most of his life in a world where everyone accepts what is, everyone lives loving, satisfying and fulfilling lives, everyone experiences and enjoys life to the full and everyone spends time exploring the possibilities that life brings.

Perhaps he'd be surprised to find there are a great many humans who know they live in a determined world but don't realise the huge benefits this knowledge can bring, and so don't use it in their day-to-day lives and have never passed their knowledge on to others.

While he might think this was the craziest planet he'd ever visited, he'd still know we humans have always done our best (the only thing we could have done), and so he'd know the bizarre behaviour he's witnessing is the only situation that could have existed right now.

Perhaps he'd stay a while to enjoy our beautiful planet and see if he could spark a change in our crazy world before thumbing a lift on a passing meteorite and continuing his journey.

TAKING ACTION

Every situation we encounter is the only situation that could have existed at that moment. But the future is another matter. The future can be influenced or changed. Our irrational tendency to wish the past or present were somehow different, or think they ought to be different or even could have been different, is matched only by our tendency to underestimate our potential to influence the future.

Certainly there are things we cannot influence. But there's a great deal we can influence or change, or help to change, in our environment, in other people and most of all in ourselves.

> *And if we want to change or achieve something in the future, we won't do it by wishing. We need to act.*

If we want a more satisfying job, career or vocation, we won't get it by complaining to ourselves about all the things that are wrong with the present one. We need to do something to make the present one better or find a new one.

If we want to study or take up a new interest, we won't do it by wishing we had more time. We need to rearrange our priorities to make more time.

If we want a new home, there's no point wishing we had more money. We need to do something to make more money.

There's no suggestion we all need a new job, interest or home. And we should be wary of thinking the grass is always greener on the other side. But if there's something we want, there's no point wishing we already had it. There's no point complaining about our current circumstances. There's no point waiting for it to happen. We need to do something to make it happen.

If we're not prepared to act, or if our priorities are such that the effort doesn't seem warranted, we need to accept our present situation to the extent we can't, or don't want to, change it.

But if when we're honest with ourselves, we find our reason for not acting has more to do with insecurity, inertia or procrastination, we need to break through these barriers (using the power tools outlined in Chapters 4 and 7) so we can have the things we want.

CASE STUDY

The world of business is full of stories of success by those who refused to give up when faced with major challenges.

When Lee Iacocca took charge of the ailing Chrysler Corporation he had no idea how bad things actually were. He knew sales were falling and as an experienced marketer he'd been brought in to turn this around.

What he found was a company with ineffective management systems, poor financial controls, inadequate systems to produce the data needed to manage the company, a not-hugely-impressive high-level management team who were far from being any sort of team, an unmotivated workforce and rapidly rising debt.

Most thought the company was doomed, which, even without all the other problems, seemed likely to become a self-fulfilling prophecy. Who'd want to buy a car from a company that was unlikely to be around long enough to manufacture the spare parts you might need?

Despite the enormous challenge, Lee Iacocca was a man who believed in the possible. He managed to turn the company around, making it once again profitable and successful.

Some might put this down to skills and ability. Those who knew him attributed his success primarily to determination and the willingness to take bold action in the face of adversity.

Here's how to get whatever you want ...
do whatever it takes.

Exercise

If there's something you want that you don't have, take a few moments to write down what you want and the steps you need to take to get it.

Decide which power tools you need to employ (Chapters 4 and 7). Write the date by which you want to have it. Decide on the first step and set a date by which you'll take it. Then do it.

Action summary

This chapter:

- Recognise nothing that's ever happened, nor any situation that exists right now, could have been different at that moment, if we were all doing our best (the only thing we could have done) given our awareness at the time, so **paccept it all**

- Understand the **future is wide open**

- If you haven't already done so, **start taking action** to create the future you desire

Prior chapters:

- Own our **reactions**

- Accept for now any uncomfortable **feelings** (fully experience and accept them)

- **Paccept** what is (our circumstances) at every opportunity

- Recognise we and others were **doing our best** (the only thing we could have done) given our awareness at the time, so paccept it

- Understand we/they are still **responsible** for our past actions, but that only impacts what happens now and in the future

- **Paccept ourselves** totally as we are, at the same time as seeking to develop

- Try to understand the other person's **perspective**

- **Take responsibility** for the way we **experience** every moment and **choose** our experience using pacceptance

- Take total responsibility for our **interactions**

- **Paccept/forgive** others

- **Reconcile** with significant others

- '**Accept** the feeling, **choose** the action' to resolve recurring feelings, unproductive habits and self-limitations

- **Commit**; stop playing the **when-then** game; **act as if**; take **bold action**; focus on **contribution**; set **goals** where needed to make changes, address goals and challenge ourselves

- Stop **worrying**

- If pacceptance and 'stop worrying' aren't enough, complete a **thought record**

- **Accept** the **feeling**, choose the **action**, challenge the **thought**

- If an uncomfortable feeling keeps recurring when you've fully accepted it, **try letting it go**

- **Observe** non-pacceptance in others (TV, etc.) and consider how you'd now think and act in their circumstances

CHAPTER 12

So you want a better world

"Nobody makes a greater mistake than he who does nothing because he can only do a little." EDMUND BURKE

If there's any aspect of the world or our environment that we'd like to change, we won't do it by wishing. Whether it's a local community issue, an issue at home or at work, a world issue such as hunger or the environment, or any other issue that concerns us:

> ### We can only make a difference if we act.

It's easy to say, 'I can't make a difference.' Often there may genuinely be nothing we can do and, if that's the case, we can accept the situation as something we cannot influence or change. But if there is something we can contribute, however small, then we surely can make a difference.

CONTRIBUTION

Instead of despairing about all the things that are wrong with the world, we can help to do something about them through our efforts, financial contribution, voicing our opinion, using our vote, or whatever.

With some issues, trying to influence the views or actions of those responsible may be one way to make a contribution. Or we can make a direct contribution ourselves. If each of us does what we can in our own way to avoid polluting the environment, we'll be making a worthwhile contribution even if the big decisions do need to be taken by governments.

But whatever the issue, and whatever the nature of our contribution, the fact remains we'll only make a difference if we act. Since others have been doing their best (the only thing they could have done) given their awareness at the time, the situation is the only way it could have been right now.

If we want it to be different in the future and others are continuing to do their best (the only thing they could be doing), our contribution is the only difference that can be made right now. Thinking that others should already be acting differently is wishing for the impossible.

WE BENEFIT TOO

I'm not for a moment suggesting we have an obligation to contribute. But making a contribution can be a source of personal satisfaction by adding meaning and purpose to our lives, as well as benefiting whatever, or whoever, we're contributing to.

> *The most satisfying lives are those that balance self-interest and contribution.*

Those who work only for the income or the recognition they receive are generally less satisfied in the long run than those who have a healthy pride in their work and a strong desire to contribute.

Taking an interest in the well-being and ultimate success of those we work with, those we work for and those who work for us, is a great deal more satisfying for most than simply viewing others and the organisation we work for in terms of how they can advance our own interests.

CASE STUDY

Susan disliked her manager. She found him demanding and disagreeable. She thought he lacked competence and yet seemed unwilling to listen to the views of others. She took consolation in the fact that she wasn't alone. Her peers thought the same and took a resistant approach towards him.

Through our work with pacceptance and her understanding that we've all been doing our best (the only thing we could have done) with the awareness we had, she began to think differently. She realised how challenging it must be as a manager to be lacking in confidence and not have the respect and cooperation of one's team.

Susan knew everyone was unhappy in the current situation. She decided to see what would happen if she adopted a more positive approach. Instead of being disagreeable towards her manager, she became more supportive. She made an effort to find out what he wanted and began to support him in achieving his goals.

The effect was remarkable. His attitude towards her quickly changed. Her peers noticed and followed suit. Their manager became less resistant and more willing to listen to advice. The team began to work together instead of in opposition and became a lot more effective. The work environment changed and became hugely more satisfying for everyone.

The same principle applies to all aspects of life. If we can find ways to contribute to others, and develop a genuine desire to do so, our own lives will be the richer for it.

Exercise

If you're employed, think of something you could do to contribute in a significant way to the person or organisation you work for, beyond carrying out your normal day-to-day responsibilities.

If you run your own business, consider how could you contribute in a significant way to your employees or your customers, beyond what is normally expected.

If you're not working, or even if you are, think about how you could contribute to your family, friends or others in a way that goes beyond what you normally do. (There are some ideas at the end of this book under the heading 'Where to from here?'.)

Whatever you're doing in life, consider how you can step beyond the norm and contribute in some significant way to others.

Action summary

This chapter:

- Find a way to **contribute** beyond your normal activities, if this is something you'd like to do

Prior chapters:

- Own our **reactions**
- Accept for now any uncomfortable **feelings** (fully experience and accept them)
- **Paccept** what is (our circumstances)
- Recognise we and others were **doing our best** (the only thing we could have done) given our awareness at the time, so paccept it
- Understand we/they are still **responsible** for our actions, but that only impacts what happens now and in the future

- **Paccept ourselves** totally as we are, at the same time as seeking to develop
- Try to understand the other person's **perspective**
- **Take responsibility** for the way we **experience** every moment and **choose** our **experience** using pacceptance
- Take total responsibility for our **interactions**
- **Paccept/forgive** others
- **Reconcile** with significant others
- Recognise nothing that's ever happened, nor any situation that exists right now, could have been different at that moment, if we were all doing our best (the only thing we could have done) given our awareness at the time, so **paccept it all**
- The **future** is wide open
- '**Accept** the feeling, **choose** the action' to resolve recurring feelings, unproductive habits and self-limitations
- **Commit**; stop playing the **when-then** game; **act as if**; take **bold action**; focus on **contribution**; set **goals** where needed to make changes, address goals and challenge ourselves
- Stop **worrying**
- If pacceptance and 'stop worrying' aren't enough, complete a **thought record**
- **Accept** the **feeling**, choose the **action**, challenge the **thought**
- If an uncomfortable feeling keeps recurring when you've fully accepted it, **try letting it go**
- **Observe** non-pacceptance in others (TV, etc.) and consider how you'd now think and act in their circumstances

CHAPTER 13

You can have it all

"Choice, not chance, determines our destiny." JEAN NIDETCH

The ideas, tools and techniques we've discussed in this book can together give us the autonomy and the power to choose our lives and our experience of life.

Having the power to choose, or the power of 'self-determination', means no longer seeing ourselves as victims of our circumstances or of other people's actions. Thoughts such as 'they did it to me' or 'life did it to me' leave us with a sense of injustice and powerlessness.

Whether we're bemoaning our ill health or fuming over other people's unreasonableness or incompetence, victim thinking takes away our power and leaves us feeling not in control of our lives.

All dissatisfaction involves, to some extent, a sense of frustration or powerlessness. When whatever has happened doesn't match our expectations or preferences, we may feel frustrated or powerless if we can't immediately do something about it, or if we couldn't prevent it.

We may not experience it as frustration or powerlessness. We may experience it as anger, fear, stress, depression, anxiety, jealousy, worry or regret. But frustration or powerlessness is usually at the root of all of these.

> *The pacceptance principle is a direct affront to victim thinking and to perpetuating the thoughts that generate a sense of frustration or powerlessness. When we choose to accept what is, and take action to change the things we can and want to change, we're taking responsibility for our lives and our experience of life.*

This book is all about taking responsibility for our lives and gaining a greater sense of our power. This isn't the sort of power we might use against others or to control others. It's the power to determine how we experience life and get what we want out of it. But it's up to us to claim that power. Nobody else can do it for us. Others can help. But the responsibility lies with us.

CASE STUDY

Jergen had reached a low point in his life. He'd lost all his money when his business collapsed.

His wife had left him and he was out of work. He felt he had no future and had even considered suicide. He was out walking one day when he passed a crippled woman pushing herself along in her wheelchair.

The woman looked up, smiled, and wished him a good day. Something clicked in Jergen's mind. Something about the significance of attitude. With some professional help, he chose to change his thinking and to approach life with a new vigour.

He later remarried and started a new business.

There are hundreds of stories of people who've experienced dramatic changes in their lives by making similar choices.

We don't need to be desperate or make dramatic changes in order to develop more productive attitudes. Earlier I suggested trying out the ideas of each chapter for at least a day or two before moving on to the next. If you've done this, your life should already have begun to change. If you chose to read the whole book first, you may still like to carry out this exercise, one chapter at a time. It should only take a month or two of practise for your life to have changed significantly.

At the end of this book, there are some more examples of ways of thinking about situations and challenges using these tools.

There's also an overall summary that you can copy and keep somewhere convenient for regular reference. You can refer to it periodically while thinking about any difficulties you may have encountered. It's helpful to review it at the end of each day and think about how it relates to your current or recent experiences and whether you've been using the tools.

The summary has been reordered to reflect, for example, that the first tool you might expect to use in a challenging situation is owning your reaction and accepting your feelings.

If there are any particular habits or patterns you want to change, make a list of these, or include them in your goals list, writing down the more positive attitudes or behaviour you'd like to adopt. Referring to the list periodically, while you look back on your recent actions, can help you absorb the ideas into your way of thinking.

AN AMAZING LIFE

It may well have been better if the past or the present had been different, but it couldn't have been different. To me this is sufficient reason to see the past and present as perfect just the way it was and is.

People often ask me if I could live my life again, would I change anything? Despite the struggles of my earlier life, despite the mistakes I've made, despite the losses and missed opportunities, I always answer truthfully that I wouldn't change a thing.

It's my life. Nothing could have been different. To want anything to have been different is to want to be someone else.

Whatever difficulties you've experienced and may be experiencing, perhaps you can see your life, both past and present, as perfect too.

The future is wide open. The future is whatever we want to make it. The future will not only be perfect, it can be amazing too if we choose to make it so.

BE TOUGH WITH YOURSELF AND GO EASY ON YOURSELF

You now have the tools to start leading an amazing life. Make sure you use them. To change old habits, it may be necessary to be tough with yourself. Decide right now that you're never again going to maintain any thought that involves wishing something were already different.

If you find yourself thinking this way, refuse to maintain the thought. Excise it from your mind while you refocus on whatever action you can and want to take to improve the future. Do the same if you find yourself worrying about the future.

Then do the same with every way of thinking and behaving that we've discussed. They're listed in the summary at the end of this book.

You won't succeed all the time, at least initially. Go easy on yourself. Even when you don't succeed you were doing your best (the only thing you could have done) with the awareness you had at the time. Change your awareness by committing to succeed next time.

START NOW

When we start taking full responsibility for our lives, we experience a greater sense of freedom and well-being. We can begin to see the world we live in as an abundant arena in which to explore our potential, whatever it may be.

We can see that who we really are – the part of us that observes, chooses and experiences – can come to no harm. Whatever may happen, as long as we're still alive, that part of us will always be able to choose how we experience life.

We can be more adventurous with our lives, explore more possibilities, be more responsive to opportunities and take more risks.

We can eliminate worry from our lives, without being any less caring or concerned. We can see there really aren't any problems to worry about; there are only people to care about, issues to think about or be concerned about, feelings to be accepted and worked through, and actions to be taken to the best of our ability. When we realise we'll always be able to choose our experience by accepting what is, we no longer need to be anxious about the future.

We can look at the difficulties and obstacles that life puts in our path as challenges through which we can grow. Without challenges, we'd simply stagnate. So we don't have to see them in a negative light. We can just paccept them as we do our best to deal with them.

We can drop our attachment to things having to be a certain way in order for us to be happy. We can choose to be more successful, wealthier or whatever else we want to be, as far as we're able to, and enjoy the benefits these things bring. But at the same time we can see we don't need these things to be happy.

Instead of needing possessions, status, abilities, success and so on in order to be able to do the things we think will bring us happiness, we can see that happiness is a state of mind that comes from healthy attitudes. When we've achieved that state of mind, we can more easily do the things we want to do and have the things we want to have.

We can be more adaptable, acknowledging that we live in an uncertain world, yet knowing we can deal with the consequences of that uncertainty as they arise. With or without healthy attitudes, life still has its ups and downs. But developing positive and productive attitudes raises the peaks, levels out the dips and makes the whole journey more enjoyable.

And while we're enjoying our own lives to the full, we can contribute freely to others and to the world we live in, in whatever ways we want to and are able to.

The promise of this book is that the pacceptance principle is a powerful tool for achieving greater happiness, satisfaction, success and fulfilment in our lives. But unless, or until, pacceptance and action are our automatic ways of thinking, we can only think in these ways if we choose to.

Choice, a simple six-letter word that reflects the power and the freedom of being human. Whatever our circumstances, we can choose to paccept what is, in our environment, in ourselves and in others, and we can choose to act in ways that will bring benefits to all. Through these choices we can take responsibility for our actions and our experience of life and claim our right to lead happy and fulfilling lives.

What more do we need than the knowledge that we have, and always will have, the freedom and the power to choose?

The summary overleaf has been arranged on facing pages for ease of copying.

I suggest you make a copy and keep it somewhere convenient for ease of reference.

As with the previous chapter summaries, you may wish to check through it at the end of each day, for a while, to see how much you've been using the tools and techniques.

As well as day-to-day events, check you're applying it to any thoughts about the past and future.

APPENDIX 1

Summary

- **Own our reactions** (we can then view our reaction and the trigger separately and paccept both)
- 'Accept for now' every **uncomfortable feeling**, without exception (fully experience and accept it)
- **Paccept** what is (our circumstances) at every opportunity
- Recognise we and others were **doing our best** (the only thing we could have done) given our awareness at the time, so paccept it
- We/they are still **responsible** for our actions, but that only impacts what happens now and in the future
- **Paccept ourselves** totally as we are (recognise we couldn't possibly have been different right now), at the same time as seeking to develop
- Try to understand the other person's **perspective**
- Take responsibility for, and exercise our power to choose, the way we **experience** every moment
- Take total responsibility for our **interactions**; the other person is doing their best (the only thing they could be doing) given their awareness right now
- **Paccept/forgive** others for their past actions

- **Reconcile** with significant others where needed

- Recognise nothing that's ever happened, nor any situation that exists right now, could have been different at that moment, as we were all doing our best (the only thing we could have done) given our awareness at the time, and so **paccept it all**

- The **future is wide open** to create whatever we wish for that's possible

- '**Accept** the **feeling**, choose the **action**' to resolve recurring feelings, unproductive habits and self-limitations

- **Commit**; stop playing the **when-then** game; act **as if**; take **bold action**; focus on **contribution**; set **goals** where needed to make changes, address goals and challenge ourselves

- Stop **worrying**: apply the pacceptance technique to the future (accept what will be to the extent we cannot control it); recognise that whatever happens we'll be able to paccept it; spot exaggerations (in probability and consequences); replace 'what-ifs' with 'then-whats'; recognise worry serves no purpose; understand worry is just a thought not reality; focus on the solution not the problem

- If pacceptance and 'stop worrying' aren't enough, complete a **thought record**

- **Accept** the **feeling**, choose the **action**, challenge the **thought**

- We can often **let go** of uncomfortable feelings once we've fully accepted them

- Find a way to **contribute** beyond our normal activities

© Graham W. Price (**www.abicord.com**; **www.body-mind-training.com**)

APPENDIX 2

More examples

Situation	Taking responsibility for my experience	Taking control
I'm embroiled in a disagreement and the other person has just said something that's irritated me	Own my reaction (my reaction is about my programming and automatic ways of thinking. After all, the other person is doing the only thing they could be doing with the awareness they have right now)	• Fully experience and accept any feelings. (Combined with owning my reaction, they'll immediately diminish) • Paccept what the other person has said (it's the only thing they could have said) • Recognise I'm the only one who can influence the situation right now (the other person is doing the only thing they could be doing) • Choose a productive response (I-statement; constructive feedback, attempt at persuasion, assertiveness; ignore it, move away, etc.)

Situation	Taking responsibility for my experience	Taking control
I've just done something I'm regretting		• Focus on, fully experience and accept any feelings • Paccept what I've done (it's the only thing I could have done) • If it's a pattern I want to break, make a commitment to do whatever it takes
I'm worrying about something in the future	• Own my reaction (I'm the one that's worrying. The situation I'm worrying about is just the trigger) • Recognise worry is just a thought, not reality	• Apply the pacceptance technique to the future • Recognise whatever happens I'll be able to paccept it • Look for exaggerations in probability or consequence • Replace 'what-ifs' with 'then-whats' • Recognise worrying has no value • Focus on the solution, not the problem

Situation	Taking responsibility for my experience	Taking control
I'm disappointed by something that's happened or a situation that exists right now	Own my reaction (my disappointment is about my programming, my automatic ways of thinking and my expectations which it turns out were in this instance unrealistic)	Paccept the situation on the basis that: • It couldn't have been different, given the awareness of everyone involved at the time • If I'm still disappointed, then acknowledge I'm wishing something were already different, recognise that's wishing for the impossible, and drop the thought • Refocus on what I can do, if anything, to improve the future
I want to achieve something that's fearful but I know is not truly risky or dangerous (i.e. it's an irrational fear)	Own my reaction (it's only fearful because of my own programming and automatic ways of thinking)	• Accept the feeling, choose the action • If necessary, make a commitment to take action • Stop playing the when-then game • Act as if • Take bold action • Focus on contribution

Situation	Taking responsibility for my experience	Taking control
I want to achieve something that's challenging (losing weight, giving up smoking, etc.)		• Paccept myself as I am right now, while I consider the benefits of change • Accept the feeling, choose the action • Make a commitment • Stop playing the when-then game • Act as if • Take bold action • Consider what the achievement could contribute to others
I'm still dissatisfied, worried, anxious or depressed despite applying these tools	Recognise my thoughts are at the core of my upset	• Identify the thought • Challenge the thought (complete a thought record) • If necessary, seek professional help
I'm grieving over a loss (someone has died, I've lost my job, I've experienced a disability, I've been robbed)	Recognise my feelings are normal	Fully experience and accept my feelings
A feeling that I've long accepted is still recurring		• 'Accept the feeling, choose the action' • Choose to let the feeling go